THE
PRAYER
LIST

Other Books by Jane Knuth

Thrift Store Saints: Meeting Jesus 25¢ at a Time

Thrift Store Graces: Finding God's Gifts in the Midst of the Mess

Love Will Steer Me True: A Mother and Daughter's Conversations on Life, Love, and God

THE
PRAYER
LIST

...AND OTHER TRUE STORIES
OF HOW FAMILIES PRAY

JANE KNUTH

LOYOLA PRESS.
A JESUIT MINISTRY
Chicago

LOYOLA PRESS.
A JESUIT MINISTRY

3441 N. Ashland Avenue
Chicago, Illinois 60657
(800) 621-1008
www.loyolapress.com

Cover art credit: iStock.com/adl21.

ISBN: 978-0-8294-4665-4
Library of Congress Control Number: 2018931304

Printed in the United States of America.
18 19 20 21 22 23 24 25 26 27 28 Versa 10 9 8 7 6 5 4 3 2 1

*Dedicated to all the praying people in my family,
especially my parents, O. Patrick and Dorothy Hudson,
and my grandparents, Vern and Lucy Hudson and
D'Arcy and Agatha Wilson. And to Aunt Kay
Donohue, who left me her amethyst rosary.*

And to St. Joseph, of course.

Contents

Prologue: The Prayer List

My aunt Kay kept the prayer list in our family. Whenever one of us needed a job, a spouse, or some surgery, she added us to it.

"I'll put you on The List," she would say, and we knew that a spiritual solution was in the works.

It required a good couple of hours each morning to get through The List, and Aunt Kay didn't tolerate freeloaders. "The List is as long as my arm," she said, clucking her tongue at us. "You let me know as soon as you hear anything, and I'll take you off it." Failure to inform Aunt Kay when a petition had been answered was grounds for sanction. If the job offer came through or the college acceptance letter arrived, and the lucky recipient didn't call her with the news, then good luck getting on The List next time. There were rewards for her demanding role. She was first in the family to be shown a sparkling new engagement ring or to get a call from the maternity ward of the hospital.

Aunt Kay was not the originator of The List; it began with her grandmother Mary Ellen Sage, an immigrant from Ireland. At Mary Ellen's funeral, all thirteen of her offspring gathered, along with the in-laws and grandchildren. The List, written in her beautiful script, was beside the casket. Her daughter-in-law Tese volunteered to take over praying in Grandma's place. Everyone in the family loved Tese, so she got the job without an argument.

After Tese "went on ahead," Cass, the eldest granddaughter, inherited The List. Her grandniece Mary (Aunt Kay's daughter) explained it this way: "Every family should have a Cass Sage: she loved children and had none of her own. She was the one who always came to stay when a new baby was born or if someone got sick. She helped everyone, and The List was right up her alley." When Aunt Kay's young husband died suddenly, leaving Kay and two children under three years old, Cass became a frequent houseguest to help out the widow.

After Cass passed, it was natural that Kay would be the next person to keep the family prayer list, which she did for most of my childhood. She prayed for me when I was reported lost on a canoe trip and while I lived in Spain. She prayed vocally whenever I drove her anywhere, especially in snowstorms. Driving isn't a natural talent of mine, so I was glad for the help.

A couple of weeks after Aunt Kay passed on, I stopped by my cousin Mary's house for a cup of coffee. She handed me a small purse and said, "Here's your inheritance." I unzipped it and peeked inside: Aunt Kay's amethyst rosary. I glanced up quickly to my cousin's sympathetic grin.

"Uh-oh," I said.

She nodded. "Looks like you're the new keeper of The List."

1

God Doesn't Give Bicycles

My husband, Dean, and I pray together every day. Well, nearly every day. We pray together in bed before we get up, except for those mornings he is traveling for work, or I wake up with a hot flash and jump out of bed at 5 a.m., or the driveway needs to be shoveled, or the phone rings, or, or, or . . . There are endless reasons not to pray.

Family prayer is not easy. Actually, family prayer is a simple thing that is hard to do. Why is that? I think it is because prayer is an intimate sharing. In prayer, we say out loud the things that worry us, or that we long to happen, or that break our hearts or bring us joy: "Lord, help me keep my temper at work today." "Help our recently widowed aunt who has cancer." "Caroline and Nick really want to get pregnant." "The tornado sirens are going off!" "We don't know how we will ever get out of debt, but *you* know how, Lord." "Thank you, thank you, thank you for the new job!" "Lord, I don't even want to forgive."

Saying these things out loud to a spouse can be more intimate than sex.

Fears, hopes, sorrows, sins, and exuberance reveal our inmost feelings and open our souls to be touched, not only by God, but also by our spouse. There are mornings when I would rather just talk to God by myself. But Dean and I have the practice of praying together, and so, even in those times, I make the effort to talk to God in front of my husband.

I am always glad I did. Praying together has never harmed our relationship, and even when one of us remains silent, or falls asleep, or qualifies the other's petition, the love grows.

We didn't begin our marriage, on the first day of the honeymoon, by praying together in bed. It wasn't something that even entered our heads in the first few years. This practice grew over time, and I give credit to our children for getting us started.

Years ago, when our two daughters were toddlers, they would climb into bed with us in the morning. We allowed this to happen just so we could catch a few more minutes of sleep. They would pat our cheeks, open our eyelids, and chatter in their baby language. Eventually, Dean would give in and start playing bouncing games or peekaboo under the covers. When everything became untucked and all hope of dozing was lost, I would murmur a morning prayer to begin the day:

> There are four corners on my bed.
> There are four angels round my head.
> Matthew, Mark, Luke, and John,
> Bless this bed that I lay on.

Little children love rhymes, and this one was a favorite of our girls. As they learned to talk, they learned the names of the four evangelists from hearing them repeated every morning and most evenings. When I mentioned to Ellen, our eldest who is now in her thirties, that I was going to try to write this book, she piped up with the "four corners" prayer from long ago, which I hadn't thought of in decades. "I still say it sometimes," she admitted. "It makes me feel safe."

When the girls were in school and the prayers stopped rhyming, we began to hear them pray things like, "Help my friend Stan get along with people at school," "Make this itchy skin go away," "It would be real nice for our family to have a puppy, Jesus."

Any petition sort of prayer can turn egoistic. It's easy to slip into asking for wants instead of for needs. And for some of us, if the answers don't come as requested, it can lead to great disappointment or loss of faith. A priest by the name of Fr. Tom gave a sermon during the years I was raising children that went something like this:

> When I was a young boy, I wanted a bike for Christmas. I prayed and prayed and prayed that this would happen. I prayed so much and so hard that I was certain that it would happen. My faith was pure and strong and unbending.
>
> On Christmas morning, I woke up full of glee and ran downstairs to look under the tree. No bike. I tried hard to hide my dismay, but I was devastated. This was no mere disappointment—God himself had let me down. After the gifts were all unwrapped and everyone was getting ready to go to Mass, my father must have noticed that I was not myself. He asked me what was bothering me.
>
> I told him, "I prayed and prayed for a bike for Christmas and God didn't give me one."
>
> He tilted his head at me and said matter-of-factly, "God doesn't give bicycles. I give bicycles. You asked the wrong person. And I'm not giving them out this year. Now go get ready for church."

This was a cautionary story for me on how to teach children to pray. I encouraged my children to ask God for absolutely anything, but I also made it clear that a gift is a gift; it's not a purchase. And God's gifts often come through other people, or the gifts affect other people's lives, so, like any good father, God's answer may be "no" or "not now," or even "ask your mother." His favors are not for sale, and he cannot be bribed with unasked-for sacrifices or with long, repetitious begging. Nor can he be threatened with abandonment if the request is not met.

But I have also observed that good fathers will sometimes allow themselves to be persuaded when their wisdom allows them to see a reason for it. In other words, even if my prayer is egoistic, God may see another reason to answer it that will bring about good for others. St. Padre Pio said:

> It is true that God's power triumphs over everything, but humble, suffering prayer prevails over God himself. It stops his hand, extinguishes his lightning, disarms him, vanquishes and placates him, and makes him almost a dependent and a friend.

Well. This is certainly encouraging for "humble, suffering" pray-ers.

But what about the ordinary family prayers we say every day, which are often neither humble nor suffering? I look on them as building a relationship with God. He answers prayers all the time, constantly listening to his children and seeing to their needs. I believe that, like any good father, he takes care of some needs before we even ask. So why do we bother to ask?

Prayer, as with most of life, is all about the relationships.

God, like any father, wants to hear from us even when we are fairly content and not looking for a handout. Like most mothers, he wants us to pick up the phone and call him regularly. Like a good friend, he wants to hang out, wasting time with us.

So Dean and I prayed daily with our daughters about the things that mattered to us and for the things that mattered to them, big or small. It was often through praying together that I came to understand what troubled them and what gave them joy. Listening to their prayers changed me and helped me become a better mother.

But when our daughters were in grade school and Aunt Kay went on ahead, and I became "keeper of The List" as my cousin called it, I had to sit up straight and think hard about how to do this. Aunt Kay had a spiral notebook full of names, and that seemed as good a plan as any, so I began that way.

First, I wrote down everyone in the family who was struggling with something. Looking it over, I felt bad about leaving people off, so I filled in the rest of the family, too, whether they needed it or not. I have a big family, and this was a long list. No wonder Aunt Kay scolded us if we stayed on it past necessity. When I sat down to pray, I mentioned everyone by name and shut the cover. I said a couple of rote prayers to formalize things and called it good.

This lasted less than a week.

It was too many names, too mindlessly said, and boring.

After a couple of months, I felt a twinge of guilt and tried writing a new page. This time I put down only the people who were really, really sick. That was much shorter. I could say a Hail Mary for each of them, and it took less time than reading the names of everyone in the family. Besides, these people needed help, so it wasn't as boring. I prayed fervently, and the feeling of accomplishment lasted for several weeks.

Then my dad's cousin died.

I had been praying for him, and he died anyway, but he was very sick and somewhat old, so it was not unexpected. I took up my pen and put a check mark next to his name. That didn't seem quite accurate, so I drew a line through his name, too.

Well. That looked heartless. *What kind of damp soul crosses out a fellow who just died?* I was no longer happy with my prayer list. I looked at everyone else on the list and pictured their names scratched out and got a queasy feeling. This list felt like a curse instead of a prayer.

Surely, Aunt Kay wouldn't have crossed out names when they died? Did she sketch stars next to the prayers that were answered? Did she doodle question marks after the ones that never seemed to resolve? Could I be overthinking this?

The scratched out first cousin once removed led me to drop the paper list for several years. I would tell family members who were bemoaning their troubles, "I'll put you on the list," but, in reality, there was no list, only an unreliable litany put together hastily from memory at the end of each day. Dean kept some names on his cell phone, but deleting those felt as wrong as crossing out the inked ones.

I felt inadequate for the job but continued doing it in this erratic way until the day came when I needed big-time prayer myself. Our family business was struggling to survive the Great Recession that began in 2008; our youngest daughter, Martha, was working in Korea, stressed and not happy; my volunteer job was interfering with increasing family responsibilities; my blood sugar was out of control; and my husband was struggling through a series of seemingly unrelated illnesses and flipping back and forth between antibiotics, steroids, and a stubborn cough.

Apparently, I needed to organize the prayer list better. I decided to begin with "thank you."

Creating a prayer list: how to begin

A prayer list is simply all the things we are asking God about. As a general rule for any prayer, it's always good to begin with "thank you." Praying on paper can make a person nervous, so for a first step try this: write a thank-you note to God. For a classic note, three lines are all you need. My mother-in-law writes the best ones I have ever read. First, she tells how great it was to hear from the giver. Next, she says what she is grateful for. Last, she tells how she plans to use the gift. Finally, she signs off with love.

Here's an example of how I write thank-you notes to God using her simple approach:

Dear God, Your sunset this evening was spectacular. You must have known how tired I was of clouds and then you sent all that purple. I texted Dean so he wouldn't miss it, and he loved it, too. Love you! Jane

Today, if you want to, begin your prayer list with a thank-you note to God.

2

Surrounded by a Cloud of Prayer

This story comes from a good friend, Barclay Shilliday, whom my husband and I have known for more than thirty years. Our families are so close that we share Christmas dinner with them most years. It's not unusual for them to be on the prayer list from time to time. One evening, we joined Barclay and his wife, Ginny, for fiddle playing and Celtic singing, and the topic of this book came into the conversation. Ginny said, "You should have Barclay tell you his dad's story from the war." Barclay has the Irish gift of storytelling, but over the course of thirty years, we had never heard about this adventure.

James Glasser Shilliday, age twenty-four, was the only child of an only child. He had no aunts, uncles, or cousins, and all his grandparents were deceased. His mother was a society lady from Pittsburgh, both an artist of note and a faithful Presbyterian. When her son joined the Army Air Force during World War II, all the Shilliday acquaintances and friends shared her alarm. They also joined her in prayer, sending letters and cards, pledging their spiritual support for the tiny family of this treasured son. "We will be praying for you and your son," the messages read repeatedly. She kept them all, tied together with a ribbon.

On September 6, 1943, James was the navigator on a B-17 Flying Fortress over occupied France in a formation of other planes returning from their targets in Stuttgart, Germany. German Messerschmitts engaged them in an impossible-to-escape dogfight that quickly turned to disaster. Two engines were hit, and the propeller flew off and busted the vertical stabilizer. The plane was flying straight but losing altitude. James and his nine fellow crew members were forced to parachute into the French countryside south of Paris near Coudray.

Destroying the American plane wasn't enough for the Messerschmitt pilots, who circled around the floating airmen, tipping the plane wings into the parachutes to deflate them and send the men plummeting to the ground. James watched, horrified, as four of his buddies perished in the blue sky. He knew he was next when, unaccountably, a thick cloud surrounded him as he floated toward the ground. It not only blocked the view of the enemy fighters but also stayed with him like impenetrable smoke from an industrial chimney all the way to the pristine farmland.

James hit the ground running, as did his other companions. Three were captured, but James and two others evaded the Germans until, eventually, the French Resistance made contact and provided them shelter in safe houses. For five months, they moved constantly from place to place, with local guides, mostly at night, always headed south toward the Spanish border. Spain was officially neutral in the war, but the people were starving because of the brutal civil war that had ended recently. This meant that arrangements with Portugal or Argentina could be made to simultaneously alleviate their food distress and help refugees escape. There was plenty of opportunity for bribery at the border crossings if the bread was fresh and the money good. During the war, the British were able to assist more than thirty thousand refugees and escaping Allied soldiers through the 160 MI-6 agents (British intelligence) stationed in Madrid.

James needed to stay free only long enough to get to that border. The five months of his journey was stop-and-go, running and waiting, filled with both boredom and terror, and all that time his mother knew only that he was listed as missing in action.

The band of soldiers met up with other refugees heading south, forged papers were acquired, and eventually the Pyrenees came into sight. One cold morning, they stood in line at a tiny border checkpoint manned by regular German soldiers who mostly wanted to go home just as they did. James was the last of his group of escapees in the line mixed in among the farmers and local families. He watched nervously as his buddies' papers were opened, glanced at, and handed back as they walked to freedom. Soon it would be James's turn, but then everything changed. A Gestapo car roared up to the checkpoint, and SS guards, in their crisp uniforms and deadly serious expressions, quickly took over the task of checking the documents and asking questions.

James's friends, already safe on the other side, stared back at him with stricken looks, but there was nothing they could do, and they all knew it. They tucked away their papers, turned up their collars, and walked away into Spain. James thought a moment about stepping out of the line and fleeing in panic, but that seemed like a horrific way to get a lot of innocent people sprayed with bullets.

Then, suddenly, almost as if he were once again suspended in his parachute over the French countryside, he felt himself being surrounded. A young child walked up and took his hand, a middle-aged woman stood directly in front of him, chatting in French, straightening his collar and buttoning his coat higher. A man and two teenage girls stepped between him and the rest of the line, subtly moving him aside so that he was no longer waiting to be checked but was instead part of an ordinary family expecting to meet someone coming from Spain to France. This cloud of people chatted, seemingly casual, including him with direct comments but not expecting any responses. The Gestapo never noticed that he had stepped out of the line.

Apparently, when it comes to prayer power, the number of people in a family doesn't matter a bit. Three clouds of protection enveloped James Shilliday and his mother during that cold year of war: the inexplicable cloud in the bullet-filled sky, the cloud of a French family, and the cloud of prayer that the society lady's friends sent in a silk-tied pile of letters.

The final letter in that pile is a telegram sent from England. It says, "Hi Mother. Having a great time. Home soon. Love, Jimmy."

I often include my worst fears on the prayer list. I tell God what keeps me awake at night and ask for his solutions.

If you want to compile a list of people to pray for, this could be a place to start. Write down the names of people you love who have the biggest needs. I sometimes sit quietly with the list on my lap for ten minutes. I picture the people and myself in knee-deep floodwaters like streets after a hurricane. I say a prayer and, while I say it, I imagine myself leading the first one to a big white rescue truck with an open back. On the tailgate, Jesus is sitting with his legs hanging down. I lift my loved one up to him, and he grabs them by the arms and hoists them into the truck, then I wade back into the water for the next person on the list. I do this until all the people are out of the muddy water and on the truck with Jesus. Then I climb up next to him and catch my breath.

On your prayer list, underneath the thank-you note, write what you most fear. Don't stop writing until all those fears are safely in God's rescue truck and you begin to feel a little calmer.

3

Like Riding a Bicycle

Everyone in this book is either part of my family, one of my friends, or a friend of my friends. It never occurred to me to advertise for family prayer stories, because my life is surrounded by praying people. Toni is one of them. She has been a member of my home parish since I was young, and I have prayed with her in committee meetings, in church, and at parish gatherings. Prayer and Toni go together.

After twelve years as a Sister of Mercy, Toni married Francis (a former Jesuit). They have two adult sons. She became a psychotherapist, retreat leader, and spiritual director. Frank's career was as professor of comparative religion at Western Michigan University.

Why am I spending time on all this background? Because knowing Toni and Frank's deep religious roots might help every parent who struggles with family prayer feel much better about themselves and their children. Here's Toni's story as she told it to me.

When Joe and Matt were young, our family prayer was simple: grace before meals, night prayer together (until they started putting themselves to bed), and Mass every Sunday. We taught them the standard prayers—the Our Father, the Hail Mary, Glory Be, and Bless Us, O Lord—along with spontaneous petitions such as "bless Grandma, bless Mom, bless Dad," and so on—typical family prayer. Frank usually led spontaneous prayer at meals. About the time the boys were school age, we started taking turns leading, but it was never forced. If one of us was flummoxed about what to say, we defaulted to the standard grace, and that was fine.

What may have been somewhat unique about our family was that the boys lived in a context of praying parents. Frank turned the original coal room in our basement into a prayer room to which he retreated regularly for silence and meditation. I surrounded a corner of the couch with my spiritual reading and the Bible and used that space daily. Our dinnertime conversations frequently mentioned contemplative prayer, so much so that when Joe was in high school, he admitted he was a little afraid to bring friends home for a meal because who knew when we might break out talking about the Holy Spirit, contemplative practices, or social justice?

One evening at supper, when the boys were in high school, all this simple, standard family prayer came to a turn in the road. There was a new chaplain at their Catholic school who had different views on social issues than Frank and I had taught them. Joe, our eldest son, said to us, "I have thought about what Father teaches us at school and about what you teach us, and I've gone up one side and down the other." He paused.

We listened.

He said, "I've decided that *there is no God.*"

How did we react? We listened some more as Joe described his struggles and conclusions.

Then, Matt, our younger son, said, "Well, I, too, have thought about these issues up one side and down the other, and I have decided that there is a God. *But the Church sucks.*"

Scroll ahead thirty years.

Joe has not attended any church through his adulthood. He married a wonderful woman, Angela, who was not raised in a faith, and they have two children: ten-year-old Sofia and her younger brother, Isaac. Matt—believer in God but distrustful of organized religion—nevertheless stayed aware of the community of faith. During his adult years, he attended several different churches. He married lovely Johanna, and they have a daughter, Kate, who is close in age to her cousin Sofia. Both young families live near me and Frank, and we find much joy in our extended family's closeness.

One day, about two years ago, Matt said to me, "Mom, Kate is becoming deeply spiritual. We have been praying with her every night, and she is asking questions that Johanna and I are struggling to answer. We were talking about how to find someone who could help her, but then it occurred to us that—duh!—we have a specialist in spirituality right in the family."

This took me by surprise, so I kept listening. Matt asked if I would consider giving Kate spirituality lessons. This was the most beautiful request I could imagine. We talked about where, when, and how long, and then I had the thought that if Kate's cousin, Sofia, also took part, the two girls would be great together. I said to Matt, "I would love to do this, but would you ask Kate if it would be OK with her if I asked Sofia to join us?" First, if it was fine with Kate, then I would go next to Joe and Angela. Matt asked his daughter, and she was all for it.

I approached Joe and Angela with the idea, and, to my delight, Angela told me about the day that Sofia was born. Angela described how, holding her daughter for the first time, the wonder of life filled her up. She had the distinct feeling that there must be something deeper to our existence than she had yet encountered. Both she and Joe said that they would ask Sofia if she would like to learn along with Kate. Sofia said yes, and that began our once-a-month, one-hour, Sunday-afternoon God sessions.

The first time we met, knowing they hadn't had any formal religious instruction, I decided to begin with any questions they already had. Kate said, "I keep hearing people talk about the Bible, but I don't know what it is." Both girls knew the Christmas story because the family celebrates it every year, and Isaac, Sofia's little brother, watches the video *The First Christmas* repeatedly. Plus, I have a collection of nativities from all over the world that are in every room of my house, so the story of Joseph, Mary, and baby Jesus was a solid place to begin. I picked up my Bible and showed them that it had two parts: the part that was written before Jesus was born, the Old Testament, and the part that was written after Jesus died, the New Testament.

I asked Sofia if she, too, had a question, and she nodded. "Is God a person or is God a spirit?" I thought, *Where did that come from?!* After a moment's stunned silence, I answered simply, "Both."

And that is where we began: What is the Bible, and Who is God? For the first year, the main focus for the beginning half of our session was "God is everywhere." The girls giggled at the thought of God under the table and in their tummies. At the beginning of our second spirituality lesson, Kate said, "If God is in all of us, then we are all connected."

I nodded. "Absolutely!"

For the second half of our time together, I let them each choose a prayer shawl from my collection of scarves and shawls, and we went down to the basement to Frank's prayer room. I used guided meditation to teach them how they might use the silence. Then, if we wished to, we shared what the quiet time was like for each of us. At the end, they each wrote in the prayer journals I gave them.

I wanted them to know that prayer can also be anywhere—just like God—so one nice day we went outside to pray under the trees in the yard. Kate threw her arms around a century-old oak and said, "This is a God-dy tree!" Sofia ran over to the redbud tree we had planted when she was born and told us, "I think this is my God-dy tree, too!"

We talked about taking time at home for prayer and quiet, and I asked them if they ever thought about doing that. They both nodded.

Kate said, "I go up to the third floor of the house where Mom and I set up a prayer place." In the past year, Kate, Johanna, and Matt joined the First Congregational Church downtown. This church provides Matt with both a support for his social justice concerns and music that is satisfying to him. He once told me that he became aware of the value of music in worship as he listened to my singing during Mass.

Sofia told us, "I go into my bedroom and pull the blanket over my head for my quiet time. And sometimes, my dad and I do quiet time together."

One time, I took them to my church in the middle of the day when it was empty. They ran around as though it were a place to explore. Sofia put her hand in the holy water font and rubbed it all over her face. "I am a queen," she said happily. Another day, I took them to an early-morning daily Mass, and afterward we had doughnuts with the others who had attended that liturgy. When they finished the sweet cakes, to my surprise, they both asked if we could return to the church so they could write in their journals.

Sure, why not?

One of the girls liked the peaceful statue of St. Joseph in the front corner of the church, so she settled there to write. The other preferred the flamboyant shrine to Our Lady of Guadalupe, surrounded with vases of flowers and lit candles. They both loved the bas-relief panel of the Last Supper that is attached to the front of the altar that holds the tabernacle. That day, Kate took a coin and tucked it into the marble frieze.

"Kate," I asked, "what is that for?"

"For someone who needs it," she said.

Sofia smiled, reached into her pocket, and pulled out and added a penny.

It took me back to all those social justice discussions at our dining table when the boys were growing up. Our sons had obviously passed on what Frank and I had given them.

This year, between Mother's Day and Father's Day, we had our annual family get-together to celebrate all the moms and dads in the family. When we gathered around our dining table, Frank asked Joe to lead the prayer. I blinked hard, but Joe didn't. He said a beautiful grace, and we went on with the celebration.

The following day, I texted Joe: *You led the prayer yesterday.*

He replied: *It's like riding a bicycle.*

In a later conversation, I told him that I was touched by his prayer. He described how, as a member of the Rotary Club, he is often asked to lead the group in prayer at their meetings. I remembered then his telling me that he sometimes led prayer with his roommates at Loyola University. "And actually," he admitted, "I sometimes find myself defending the Catholic Church in discussions when criticism points that way. When people ask me what I am, I tell them I'm Catholic. I value its sense of mystery. But I can't go with organized religion." He has also let me know that he sometimes feels the presence of the One beyond us when he sits quietly outside. He has come to the awareness of how little we know of God while knowing God.

My sense of all this is that there is no determining how the Spirit is going to lead any of us. I rejoice in the goodness I see in my sons. I know that God is there. And I think our rather simple family prayer has had something to do with it all.

Perhaps some of our family members are not comfortable in church. Maybe some of them do not like to pray out loud at the table.

Sometimes we pray on the living room sofa or in a quiet basement room, and sometimes we pray in a dinnertime discussion of social justice or in an empty church. Toni taught me that family prayer can happen on the third floor of the house or with our arms stretched around a tree.

Or even huddled together with a blanket pulled over our heads.

Look around at the place in which you have chosen to pray. Why here? Where else do you love to pray? Do you have a family member who prefers to talk with God outside organized religion? Where do they pray? Add them to your prayer list if you haven't already.

4

Prayer Perseveres

Theo and Mira emigrated from Bulgaria, where they often played a card game called belot, *which has some similarities to euchre, a classic Midwestern game. When they moved to Michigan, they needed friends, and the time-honored method of sitting around a square table, trying to outwit one another with cards, helped them find their way into our home and our hearts. Dean and I have been euchre buddies with them for nearly twenty years. Theo and Mira are atheists, so when I told them about the topic of this book, they surprised me with their enthusiastic response. "Theo's mother prays for us," Mira said. "She never forces it; never insists. It's always something like, 'Don't worry, I'll pray'—very simple." In this chapter, Theo tells about his mother, Bistra, professor of Bulgarian literature, author of more than 250 publications, and a woman of prayer.*

I grew up in communist, atheist Bulgaria with a very religious mother. The churches were allowed to exist, the buildings were left standing, and people could attend the Orthodox services, but very few did so. Officially, it was fine to go to church. Unofficially, it was not fine. Belonging to a church was a sure path to a dead-end career and possible arrest and imprisonment. But my mom, Bistra, was not intimidated by the government authorities. Throughout my childhood, she attended church every Sunday all by herself so as not to impose the risk she was taking on my father (a complete atheist) or my younger brother and me. My father was afraid for her, but he didn't make her stop going to church.

Why wasn't she arrested? Why did she retain her prominent position as a professor at the university? *Because she was that good at her work.* From first grade through her postdoc, Bistra never earned a B on any quiz, test, paper, or class. She was proficient in five languages, and throughout the Balkan Peninsula her work was well known and admired. Following is Bistra's remembrance of the communist years.

The Atheistic Past
by Bistra Gancheva

As time passes, fewer and fewer people remember the religious oppression during communism. Religion, known as the "people's opiate," was treated as a harmful lie that needed to be constantly fought against. And even though churches existed and were functional, religious oppression was universal.

In Bulgaria, the worst wasn't the actual repression (as bad as that was). The worst was the mass, government-supported ideology that any true Christian is a "victim" or a "carrier" of misguided beliefs, and that he or she is spiritually undeveloped and suspicious. And although the constitution officially allowed any Bulgarian citizen to carry on with religious acts, simply visiting a church could lead to serious consequences. To this day, I am not able to explain to myself how my parents were able to sow the seeds of faith in me given the external circumstances.

One example: when I was in high school, a schoolmate of mine passed away. Everyone who knew him was convinced that he was a great person. Weeks after his death, it was unbearable going into our classroom; nobody was able to concentrate on studies.

He was the son of a pastor, and his funeral had to be a religious one. I remember the father: a frail old man who walked in front of the casket, not hearing everyone's cries.

The funeral procession, which included the whole school, stopped in front of the church. No student or teacher dared go inside. The principal stood in front of the church door, making sure no one joined the proceedings inside. And sadly, we couldn't blame him. Had a student or a teacher been spotted inside the church, the principal would have been accused of a "blatant error in the fight against religious misconceptions." Who would have acted differently?

At the very end of the funeral, when others were unable to contain their grief, the father crossed himself quietly. The next day, all comments revolved around how the one who should have been hurt the most had looked the calmest. He had actually done the simplest act of faith, however difficult it was to comprehend even for religious people: he had accepted a higher power capable of absorbing all human pain or joy.

This is why, later, as a college student, I looked for remote churches, away from the prying eyes of the establishment. In the Alexander Nevski Cathedral in Sofia (where any visit could be seen as historical or artistic) I tried to find an obscure corner, so I would not be seen. The complex architecture of the building does afford a few places suitable for private prayer.

In this way, a long time passed without any hope for change in Bulgaria. Change, however, finally came.

Theo continues the story about his own upbringing.

I went to regular Bulgarian school and was taught what the communist government wanted us to learn: that there is no God. My mother made the decision not to convey her religious beliefs to me because she knew the dangers involved, but she raised me with the spirit of Christianity. I was brought up with those values, but I was never taught the "why" of them. The arguments against religious belief I learned in school made sense to me, and I would sometimes push my mother: "Mom, there is no way Jesus can walk on water!" She was so eloquent (a classical literature professor) and peaceful and confident that she could actually explain to me why it was entirely possible that Jesus walked on water. Yet, still, she never imposed her beliefs on me.

The communist government fell in 1989, a few years before I was ready to go to college, and things began to change. I was a soccer player, and Bistra was a huge fan of the sport. She could talk about all the teams and their players. In 1990, there was a nationwide contest for one young soccer player from Bulgaria to win a sport scholarship to attend college in the United States. This was a huge dream of mine, and I competed fiercely for it, but I came in second. The winner had connections with a government official, and the old system was still enough in place that the outcome was rigged.

I was completely crushed by the results.

My mother saw my profound disappointment and decided that nothing was more important to her than my happiness. She wrote letters to the Bulgarian ambassador to the United States, employing all her eloquence and outrage. The result of her campaign was that the rules of the contest were changed, and *two* of us were given scholarships to go to the States. It was the beginning of all the opportunities I have had in my career, but it was the end of my life in Bulgaria. My mother wanted me to have my dream more than she wanted me to stay close to her. She is an amazing woman.

After graduation, Mira and I settled in the United States, where our daughter, Zizi, was born in 1999. Every summer we sent Zizi back to Bulgaria to spend a month with each of our families. We wanted her to know her grandparents, aunts, uncles, and cousins, and also the Bulgarian language. But early on, it became clear that she needed to learn not only how to speak the language but also how to read and write it, so we asked Bistra if she would teach her. Bistra was happy to do this, and each summer when we traveled back to fetch her home, Zizi would be using Bulgarian like a native.

When she was a second grader, the other kids in her class in the United States became aware that Zizi spoke another language. They sometimes asked her to talk in Bulgarian, and one time, when Mira was present, Zizi recited the entire bedtime prayer that is commonly taught to children in the Orthodox Church in Bulgaria.

Mira was astonished and said, "You know that prayer? How? We didn't teach you that."

Zizi said, "Grandma taught me." And she knew other prayers and Bible stories, as well.

It turned out that Bistra, released from the communist oppression, had employed the Bible and prayer books to teach her granddaughter the Bulgarian language. But with her usual integrity, she never imposed the beliefs on Zizi. In Zizi's mind, she was learning Bulgarian. Bistra passed on her native tongue using the stories of her faith, but she respected Mira and my belief that a person can have good values without being religious.

Where does this story of persevering faith go from here? Ten years ago, after forty years of marriage, my father converted to Christianity. He is more converted than anyone I have ever met—an enthusiastic believer.

Again, Bistra takes up the story from Bulgaria . . .

. . . and the Different Future
by Bistra Gancheva

My husband's path to finding God was different. He wrote himself about the fruitless, atheistic years of his youth. In his open letter to Dan Brown, the famous author, published in the *National Church Newspaper*, he contends that Brown is just arriving where he is coming back from.

For a long time, everyone in the family lived with their own beliefs without imposing them on anyone. My husband's tolerance of my church visits could have really cost him (and us) dearly, but he never explicitly told me that. And now we go to church together.

Today, things are different. Eastern Orthodox liturgies are now legal, and Christmas and Easter celebration Masses are televised from the same Alexander Nevski Cathedral where I once hid.

The only thing we could not do was convey the beginnings of faith to our children the way they were conveyed to me by my parents. Instead of being a part of our children, Christianity is more of an ideology among many others. This is why I would say that their disposition toward faith is one of a positive distancing.

I never stop praying that every one of my children finds his own illuminated, sacred path to God. There are many such paths, but my children can follow only their own initiative and convictions. God's will, however, is above all.

Bistra is loved and admired by her family even though her faith is hard for them to understand. She never made them feel guilty or

lacking, and after decades of prayer, her husband found God. Today, Bistra perseveres in prayer for her children and grandchildren.

Write today about the specific joy that your faith gives you, and then add to your prayer list the names of people whom you long to share in that same joy.

5

Amazing Grace

My older brother Patrick plays the bagpipes. His entire neighborhood knows about his hobby by virtue of the weekly practice sessions he conducts on his back porch. Bagpipes are not an indoor instrument. He plays the pipes at parades, festivals, weddings, and funerals.

Every year on Memorial Day, Patrick and his wife, Gina, pick up my mom at her place and drive to the cemetery where my grandparents, our dad, and Aunt Kay are buried. Gina tends the flowers while Patrick takes the pipes out of the case, puts them together, and tunes up the drones. They all stand over the spruced-up graves and pray the Hail Mary, the Our Father, and the Glory Be, and petition mercy for "their souls and all the souls of the faithful departed."

Then Patrick plays the pipes.

Families scattered about the cemetery visiting the graves will stop what they are doing to listen. Bagpipes are a type of prayer that doesn't always stay within our clan.

One Saturday in late fall, Patrick was having trouble figuring out the fingering for "Amazing Grace," which led to quite a few repetitions of the melody with all the drones bellowing, until one of the neighbors had had enough for the day and politely told him so over the fence. Patrick apologized, packed his instrument into its case, and drove twenty miles away to the family lake cottage. The neighbors on both sides of the property were Upper Peninsula natives and wouldn't appear again until spring, so the bagpipes were unpacked, and the practice resumed with little risk of bothering anyone. It was a perfect place and a perfect day to set the melody free over the expanse of water.

Several weeks later, a story circulated around the lake and eventually found its way to Patrick.

A longtime resident of the lake from across the bay had been living under hospice care for several weeks. He breathed his last with his wife and family surrounding his bed, peacefully going on ahead to an even more beautiful place than he was leaving. The death certificate was signed, and the funeral home was called. They sent a van with two attendants, who transferred the gentleman to a gurney and wheeled him out the door. As the family followed the stretcher into the autumn morning, the strains of "Amazing Grace" swelled across the water. The attendants, startled, glanced at one another and stopped in their tracks. Everyone's gaze searched the shores of the lake looking for the source, but there didn't seem to be anyone about.

The procession paused for the entire length of the hymn. When the last echoes faded away, the family smiled through their tears and finished the walk to the van.

A bothered neighbor, and a piper unaware of how God was using him, together combined with God's perfect timing to bestow amazing mercy.

✎ **Family prayers can be for complete strangers. When I was a child in school, if a siren sounded, the nuns who taught us would stop class and have the entire class pray together for whoever needed the siren. I still do this, and I taught my daughters to do it. We typically say, "Lord, please help whoever is part of that siren." This** includes the person in need—who could be experiencing the worst day of his or her life—the family members, and the rescue personnel.

Include a person or group of people on your prayer list who are in need, even if you don't know them.

6

One of the Family

Debbie came to a talk I gave at her church about the Society of St. Vincent de Paul. After telling of my experiences meeting Jesus in the people at a thrift store, several of her fellow parishioners came to me afterward and said, "You ought to meet Debbie. She has the best story." I asked to be introduced to her, and they were right. Debbie taught me about family prayer that reaches out and includes our eternal family. She and her daughter were on my prayer list for a long time.

Debbie is the custodian at three Catholic churches. If you walk into one of her buildings, you will know it by the way the old linoleum tiles on the floor gleam.

When he was in his forties, Debbie's husband died of throat cancer. At the moment of her husband's passing, the parish priest stopped by the hospital room and gave the last rites. When he was finished, he asked her if there was anything else he could do for her.

"Yes," Debbie replied, "I promised to pray an hour of adoration this afternoon for a friend who is sick. Could you do it?" He could, and he did.

During her husband's illness, the little family had prayed like never in their lives. Their prayers brought them closer together and closer to God than Debbie had thought was possible. "In some ways, my husband's cancer saved our lives. It saved our souls because we had never learned to depend on God before that happened. With the cancer—all we had was God and each other."

All during the funeral preparations, the visitation, and the ceremony, Debbie had been the one who gave comfort and consolation to others. She was the one lavishing the smiles and the hugs on everyone else.

Several days later, after the funeral, the burial, and the luncheon, and after the gathered friends and family had gone home, Debbie and her teenage daughter were alone in their house. During the many months of treatments and sickness, Debbie had been brave and calm for her husband and her daughter.

But at that point, her life shattered. Simultaneously exhausted and unable to sleep, Debbie felt anger at God well up inside. She grabbed blankets and pillows and told her daughter to get in the car. They drove to her home parish church. All the lights were out and the doors locked, but Debbie, as custodian, had a key. They went into the church and, on one of the back pews, she created a makeshift bed for her daughter and told her to go to sleep because they might be there for a while. She had some things to say to God, and she would wait for an answer.

With her daughter taken care of, Debbie walked up the main aisle of the sanctuary and stood directly in front of the altar. "I crossed myself, genuflected; you know the routine—I was mad, but I wasn't rude—then I looked directly at that image of Jesus on the cross and I said to him, 'All right, you took my husband and I'm damned mad about it. I'm not too happy with you. I don't even like you. But,' she teared up, 'you're part of the family . . . so I guess I'll have to deal with you anyway. That's what family is.'"

She walked up to the crucifix and put her hand on Jesus' nailed feet. And then, in a moment of clarity, Debbie knew: *it was okay.*

It wasn't all better, her life would never be the same again but—*it was okay*. She didn't know how it was okay, but she was suddenly certain that it was.

At that moment, a cool breeze passed over her head and moved her hair. Her gaze left the figure on the cross and looked around in every direction. Debbie knew the architecture and systems of that church like no one else—she was the maintenance person. There was no source, no reason, for the air movement. In the back of the church, her daughter sat up and said, "It's cold in here, Mom; there's a breeze. Let's go home."

"I have the best job in the world," Debbie says. "I go to work every day, and whenever I'm having a tough time, whenever I need to, I walk in here and talk to Jesus."

On your prayer list, tell God about a prayer that wasn't answered the way you wanted. Ask questions about that. After you write your questions down, sit silently and hold them for ten minutes. Set a timer and close your eyes. Rest with the questions.

7

Merciful Prayer

Shortly after my first book, Thrift Store Saints, *was published, I arrived home after a tiring day, started cooking supper, and checked the answering machine for messages. While I stirred onions and peppers in the pan, half listening to the telemarketers and appointment reminders, a woman's voice spoke hesitantly through the machine.*

"My Name Is Susan . . ."

"Hello, Jane, my name is Susan. You don't know me, but I had to call you and tell you something. I read your book, and that story in chapter three about the woman who couldn't forgive her father—that really struck my heart. She talked about how people told her she wasn't a Christian unless she could forgive everyone, but her father had abused her, and she had left home when she was fourteen. The end of her story, where she described how Jesus was on the cross and he prayed for the people who were killing him, and he didn't specifically forgive them, but he said, '*Father*, forgive them.' Oh, wow. He prayed for his killers. He asked God to forgive them. I read that, Jane, and I thought, *I can do that. I can pray for my ex-husband. Even if I can't forgive him, there is no reason I can't pray for him.* Anyway, I just had to call you and tell you how much that story changed my heart. I will be praying. And I am so grateful. Goodbye, Jane."

I turned off the stove and saved the message on the machine. I will never forget Susan, who found the strength to pray for her ex-husband.

Mercy in the family is a sign that relationships matter more than being right, more than money or possessions, and more than hanging on to our hurts. "Seven times seventy times" is just about the right number of opportunities that family members are given to forgive one another over the years. Mercy and forgiveness require lots of prayer. We are not capable of forgiving big hurts by ourselves because our love is too small. But God is invincible. He can forgive the gravest of harm when we cannot. Some say that praying to God to forgive our loved one is the path to being able to forgive that person ourselves.

Susan walked that path.[1]

It is important to pray for troubled family relationships, but it is more important to leave the relationship before violence destroys a soul or body.

The next story is about family mercy and forgiveness that took a long time.

After noticing Liz for a couple of years in church, I finally met her. She's the type of "church lady" I remember from my childhood: perfectly arranged white hair, shoes that match her dress, a minister of the Eucharist, visitor to nursing homes and hospitals, and (where I met her) a volunteer for emergency food distribution in the neighborhood. Once or twice a month for two years, she and I worked side by side packing tomatoes, dividing up frozen potatoes, and prying open No. 10 cans of peaches. To me, she seemed like a prime example of a typical constant

---

1. Of course, in the case of abusive behavior, where forgiveness is doled out over and over again but the bad behavior only returns and escalates, the relationship that we are trying to save may just kill us. Giving mercy to an abuser is not family prayer. It is beautiful to forgive another person, but there is no beauty in allowing someone to repeatedly harm us either physically or psychologically.

Catholic—she even led our group in prayer before we put on our hairnets and aprons—so I wasn't expecting the reply she gave when I asked her if she had any family prayer stories.

"You Will Have Other Things You Will Be Doing"

"I didn't pray at all for forty years," Liz said matter-of-factly. "In all that time, I seldom walked into a church and I never received communion."

My jaw probably hung open for a second. *"Forty years?!"*

She nodded. "I was eleven, the youngest in the family, when my father was killed by some drunken teenagers in a head-on car crash. I was filled with rage at God and at my mother. I couldn't believe that she could possibly miss my dad as much as I did, so whenever I saw her crying I would seethe with resentment. Why was she crying? I was the one who lost my father!"

"Before my father died, our family used to pray regularly together on our knees on the cold floorboards of the old farmhouse. His death was the end of family prayer. I'm not sure about my brothers and sisters, but I just stopped. I know my mom still prayed. She prayed the rest of her life for all of us to have the gift of faith and—in my case at least—it worked. It took forty years, though."

Liz wiped tears from her cheeks. "I treated my mom terribly while I was growing up. We used to have raging arguments, and I mourn the awful things I said to her. She must have understood how much pain I was carrying because she never gave up on me. Eventually, when I grew up, we put together a good relationship."

"How did that turn around?" I asked.

"I'm not sure. Maybe her prayers? My mom prayed a lot. I remember that, a few months before she passed away, she asked me to go with her on an errand. I didn't know where we were going until we ended up at the funeral home. She had made an appointment to prearrange her funeral. I sat there numbly while she picked out the casket, arranged the visitation, and paid for the whole thing. When we finally left the place and climbed into the car, I said: 'That's the most awful thing you have ever asked me to do. Didn't you think us kids could have done that for you after you're gone?'"

Even though I was distressed, she was calm. "No," she said. "You'll have other things you will be doing."

"Like *what*?"

"Crying," she answered.

"And the day she died, I *was* crying. I had to drive home on the highway from a town twenty miles away, and I couldn't think straight—probably driving wasn't a good idea. I didn't know what to do, but while I was driving, I heard a voice say, 'You just keep praying, and it will come to you.' I was flabbergasted, but it made me feel a little better. Just before I arrived home, I clearly heard my mother's voice say, 'May the good Lord bless and keep you.'"

"I thought, *What does that mean? Is that a hymn?* I went into the house and looked up the hymn. It was a song made popular by Kate Smith from a long time ago. The words were perfect. They were just the kind of thing my mom would say to us. I read those lyrics at her funeral, and I am certain that it was only because of Mom's prayers that I could read them to my brothers and sisters."

"My father's death was why I left God behind. My husband's death and my mom's prayers brought me back."

This is a story about mercy and stolen family photos. It is from a friend who showed me how to pray for people instead of outcomes.

Mercy and Grace

I am sure that no man asks mercy and grace with sincerity,
without mercy and grace being given to him first.
—Julian of Norwich

Shortly before Thanksgiving, while she was volunteering at a thrift store, my friend Grace's wallet was stolen out of her purse. She had a suspicion that the wallet walked away with a man who had been in the vicinity earlier in the day, but there was no evidence, and so she couldn't accuse him.

"But," she says, "I decided I could pray for him." In addition to praying, Grace went about the business of reporting all the items missing: credit cards, driver's license, and cash. The police gave her little hope of ever seeing the wallet or the photos of her grandchildren again. "That only gave me more reasons to pray for the thief," she says.

Several weeks passed, and Grace traveled out of town for a short trip. When she returned, there was a postcard from the US Postal Service in her mailbox asking her to call, so she did.

"We have your wallet," the clerk told her. "Someone dropped it in a mailbox. Bring some ID and you can pick it up."

"I was so excited," says Grace, "that I drove there the next day. My wallet was in perfect condition, not dirty or scuffed at all. Even better, everything except the cash was inside it: the driver's license, the cards, and most important—my grandchildren's pictures. And behind the kids' photos, the twenty-dollar bill I keep for emergencies was still there. The thief obviously didn't search through my things because everything was where I usually store it. I guess he only needed some extra cash."

Julian of Norwich says that God's mercy is so great that he grants it before we even ask for it. Grace is so confident in this that she asked for mercy for the thief without a hope that she would see her wallet again. Our elders have much to teach us about prayer.

On your prayer list, tell God about something you are struggling to forgive.

Write the person's name. Maybe, like Liz, it is God you find hard to forgive. If you are ready, ask God to be merciful to you and to whoever else needs it. If you aren't ready, don't push yourself—just write it on your prayer list. Instead, pray to be *ready* to forgive someday.

8

Come, Lord Jesus, Be Our Guest

Dean and I are an interdenominational couple; he is Lutheran, and I am Roman Catholic. When we began our married life, the first evening in our new home, we faced each other across the dinner table and paused. *Which meal grace should we say?* Dean's family had a retinue of half a dozen grace-before-meals, but I had inherited only one: "Bless us O Lord, and these thy gifts, which we are about to receive from thy bounty through Christ, our Lord. Amen."

We made the decision on that first evening to pray in our own words, saying in plain English what we were grateful for and asking God's blessing on the food. That worked fine for a few years, until our first child, Ellen, began sitting at the table with us. We lived near both sets of grandparents and ate with them regularly. Ellen needed to know their mealtime prayers so she could recite them with the extended families. So, we began saying the various Lutheran prayers at breakfast and lunch and the Catholic prayer at supper. One of these is quite short and became a favorite. It goes like this:

"Come, Lord Jesus, be our guest, and let this food to us be blessed."

Ellen and her sister, Martha, learned it quickly and said it speedily, especially when they were hungry. One day, after finishing the prayer, four-year-old Ellen asked me, "Mama, what's *beourguest*?"

"Sorry?" I said, while cutting her sister's meat. "What did you say?"

"Beourguest. What's beourguest?" she said patiently. "Come, Lord Jesus, Beourguest. I know Jesus, but I don't know beourguest."

"Oh, dear!" I chuckled. "We are saying, 'Be. Our. Guest.' It's three words, not one word."

Dean explained that we were inviting Jesus to come sit at the table with us, like company. "We want him to bless our food and be with us while we eat."

Ellen and her little sister exchanged pensive looks, and then Martha, age three, said, "But there's no place for Jesus to sit. And NO PLATE!"

Dean smiled indulgently and walked over to the kitchen cupboard. "You're right. We should have a place for Jesus." He fetched a plate and pulled an empty chair to the table. Both girls smiled and began eating again.

After a couple of minutes, Ellen said, "Jesus doesn't have a cup."

Dean interrupted his meal again and brought a sippy cup to the table.

Martha liked this game. "He needs a spoon, too! And a fork!"

My indulgence wore thin. "Jesus eats with his fingers. That's how they do it in the Bible all the time. He doesn't use silverware."

"Oh." They nodded seriously. "Even soup?"

"Even soup. He's God. He can do amazing things."

After that, we always had a place at the table for Jesus. Our daughters were happy to know he was there, and Dean and I found the extra plate to be a good reminder, too.

A few months into this practice, Dean began carpooling to his job with a coworker, Steve. One morning, Steve stopped by our house before Dean was ready, so we waved to him from the porch to come inside. While I fed the children and Dean packed his computer bag, I asked Steve if he would like an English muffin, which he accepted.

Both girls stopped eating and stared at him with new interest as I put the muffin in front of him. When he sipped his coffee and spread jam on the bread, Ellen asked boldly, "Are you Jesus?"

Steve blinked at her. "Excuse me? Am I *Jesus*? Why would you ask that?" Dean fumbled his bag and stared at our young daughter.

Martha nodded and said, "You're sitting in Jesus' place. Are you Jesus?"

Steve leapt out of the chair in confusion while Dean and I tried to explain the prayer to him between gasps of laughter. The girls weren't sure if this was appropriate. They were entirely serious. We eventually sorted out Steve's identity for them and found a new place for him to sit down.

Dean and I learned from this that, for children at least, prayer is not a mere formality. If an invitation to God is sent out, then why wouldn't he show up at the table? For them, God is not abstract. He is as real as a stranger eating an English muffin.

✎ **Write your favorite childhood prayer. Then read it out loud to God.**

9

Tradition as Family Prayer

One of the curious things about my family's prayer list is that it has been passed down for five generations. Somewhere along the way it became family tradition. This chapter is about my friend, a German immigrant who came to the United States in 1937, fleeing Hitler before the beginning of World War II. Her family brought many traditions from her homeland and uses them as tangible ways to pray with children and others. Following is the story of how her family celebrates Advent and Christmas.

We have to learn to wait for things; we wait for spring, we wait for the sunrise, we wait for time to pass, and one of the things we need to learn to wait for is Christmas. Traditions help us wait. In our tradition, a week into Advent, we celebrate St. Nicholas's feast day on December 6, then there is St. Lucy, St. Barbara, Our Lady of Guadalupe, the Immaculate Conception—Advent is full of celebrations, and all of them are preparations for what is coming. My husband and I didn't tell the kids that Santa was coming, nor did we take them to visit the department store's Santa—it wasn't in our tradition. It was our tradition to wait for the Christ child. That huge, long buildup that commercial Christmas has become seems like unnecessary torture to me. Why wait so many weeks?

On December 6, the eve of St. Nicholas, we set empty plates at our places at the table and sing the good saint's song: "Nicholas was a very good man, tra-la-la-ley, happy, happy, happy, tra-la-la-ley, tomorrow is St. Nicholas's Day!" In the morning, when the children wake up, all the plates are piled high with sweets. The biggest and best is a *spekulatius* (speculoo, or spice) cookie in the image of St. Nicholas himself. Next to the plates are three oranges, which represent the three bags of gold that Nicholas threw over the wall to save the impoverished girls. The children hear us retell the stories of this holy bishop who cared so much about young people, poor children, and redemption for sinners. This is the beginning of our preparation for Christmas, but it isn't only a cute custom: it is about the joy of selfless, secret giving. When our oldest kids went away to college, they were living in dormitories on St. Nicholas Day, so without hesitating, they made cookies, tied them with ribbon, and hung them on the doors of their friends' rooms in the dead of night. This wasn't something I told them to do; it was their giving hearts that shared the tradition of secret giving.

During the four weeks before Christmas, my family has a long tradition of placing an empty manger in the center of our Advent wreath. Next to it, in a tidy bundle, we keep short pieces of clean straw. The children may place one piece of straw in the little crib for every act of kindness or sacrifice that they make. This is typically done on the honor system, and the straw bedding grows little by little through the weeks to make baby Jesus a nice soft bed when he comes on Christmas Eve. Each Sunday of Advent, we light a new candle on the wreath. As the days shorten and become darker, the progression of light from the wreath grows until it explodes in the lights of the Christmas tree. This step-by-step journey of small sacrifices, bits of straw, and candlelight combine to show our love for one another and for Jesus.

Once, one of the littlest asked me, "How come you and Dad never put straw in the crib?"

Okay. Fair enough. So that year, we adults began adding straw, too. Then the children asked, "Why don't we all say what we did at the end of the day during family prayer time?"

I grew up *not* saying; it was a private matter. But when my kids asked, "What have you done?" then it became a family prayer. The tradition changed because it needed to change. That's the thing about tradition: it can grow from generation to generation.

In the German tradition, it is the Christ child Jesus who brings not only the gifts but also the tree and all the decorations as well. Early in the day on December 23, my husband and I set up our tree in a corner of the room behind a curtain. It is very mysterious, the house becomes quiet, and no one is allowed to touch the curtain or peek behind it. The children can place the presents they have for one another next to the curtain, but no closer. I spend the day decorating and baking sweet bread called stollen, and as each batch comes out of the oven, my husband takes the children and the pastry and they deliver it, in long circuitous routes, to friends and neighbors. While they are gone, I sneak behind the curtain to decorate and stash presents under the tree, including the ones the kids have left near the curtain, then I go back to the kitchen and decorate more bread. By the end of the day, all the bread gets delivered and the children come home. On Christmas Eve we have a simple supper and then we go upstairs to a bedroom to read Christmas stories together. After the stories, we sing songs and read the biblical Christmas story, waiting for the Christ child to come, all the while listening for the sound of the Christmas bell. Suddenly, the tinkling is heard! We start to sing "Oh, Come Little Children" in German and process down the stairs. But alas! No one is there. Then we run over to the curtain, pull it away, and behold all the lovely gifts around the decorated tree shining with lights. Everything in the room is transformed!

Over the years, this elaborate plan eventually involved a neighbor who sneaked up onto the porch to ring the bell at the right time. Our friends would vie with one another over who would be the bell ringer. One young man, on a snowy evening, pasted himself to the outside wall of the house and shimmied all the way around until he could climb onto the porch railing without leaving a single footprint in the snow. Our kids were teens by then, and they went wild trying to figure out how that bell rang.

The best part of this elaborate staging of Christmas is that, when the curtain is flung back and the gifts and tree are revealed in all their glory, the first thing the children look for is the crib. The baby Jesus has finally arrived and is sleeping in his comfy padding of straw that they have carefully piled piece by piece during Advent. "Look!" they say, "Feel the straw. Is there enough to make a soft bed?" Then, they all gather together and recite the Christmas prayer they have been memorizing during Advent. We use the lyrics of "In the Bleak Midwinter," and when the kids come to the part about "What shall I give him? Give my heart," it is sweetly dramatic. One year, our five-year-old son pulled a scrap of pink cloth from his pocket and said, "I made this blanket for Jesus because the straw is so prickly." We used it every year after that.

These traditions are all family prayer because we are talking about God and talking to God through it all and including the children.

One of my favorite Christmas memories is when my oldest daughter was three years old. On St. Nicholas Day (which is also her birthday), she received a gift of one dollar in a card from my husband's mother. On December 23, I took her to the five-and-dime store and allowed her to choose whatever she wanted. She wandered all over the store, looking at everything until she came to the stocking section in the back of the store. She picked out a long pair of bright red knee-highs, much too large for her. Both the clerk and I tried to tell her that they wouldn't fit, but she was not to be argued out of it, so that's what we bought.

That evening, some neighbors came by the house and reported that a house had burned down in the neighborhood, and they were going to take a small gift to the family who was preparing to be transported to the homes of relatives. Our daughter wasn't feeling well—feverish and already in bed, but she said, "Take them my red socks!" and she insisted. They added the socks to their gift and went to the unfortunate family's place.

The cars were already outside ready to take the family away. The Red Cross had brought clothing for the children, who had only the clothes they were wearing when they rushed out to safety. The oldest daughter, a teenager, was barefoot—no shoes or socks, and there weren't any for her in the Red Cross bags. The red knee-highs were presented to her, and she was relieved to cover her feet in the cold air. They fit her perfectly.

On Christmas morning, my daughter opened a package that had arrived from my mother several days earlier. Inside was a pair of bright red socks, just exactly her size. She hugged them tight and refused to open any other packages. "I got my dollar on St. Nicholas Day, and he knew already that I needed big socks. And today, he made sure I got some to fit me!"

Traditions deserve respect, just as prayer deserves respect. They are all wrapped up in what people believe, and there isn't only one way to believe. Keeping family tradition is important, and being open to other people's tradition is important, too.

Do you have a tradition you keep that involves prayer? Maybe you have traditions, but the prayer is missing. Can you think of a way to add it?

10

"Don't Ever Stop Praying"

Free your mind from all that troubles you;
God will take care of things.
—St. Vincent de Paul

When Dean and I were in the middle of the multiple crises I mentioned earlier, our morning prayer began to take on a feeling of futility. Each day, we prayed the same things: "Lord, please help us find a way out of the business debt; the pressure of overwork is grinding down everyone in the family—help! Dean's cough keeps getting worse; show me how to keep from being anxious about it all; and please help Martha—she's so far away!"

Each morning, we put it all in God's hands and loaded it onto his rescue truck, and the next day it felt as if it were all back in the flooded streets. So, by using prayer, we hoisted it back onto the tailgate. It seemed like an endless loop, and occasionally I wondered whether my time could be better spent. But regardless of the non-improvement, we kept praying. I can't say that we prayed hopefully; it was more helplessly. We didn't have any other options.

During this time, I met a man at the St. Vincent de Paul thrift store who taught me that family prayer is a means rather than an answer.

This man and his fiancée were praying people. They both came from poverty and broken homes, but they had met each other in church, and prayer lifted them up out of their respective pasts. They wanted to do things the right way this time, the way God wanted.

They decided that, before planning a wedding, to which they would invite all their friends and family to celebrate with them, they needed good jobs. So, they prayed about that and put it before the Lord. They also needed stable transportation, and they put that on their prayer list, too. They prayed deliberately, purposefully, and consistently. And it all happened, little by little, over several months. First the jobs, then they saved their money for a good car, and at last the time was perfect and they planned the wedding. They told the minister, hired a caterer, and sent out dozens of invitations.

That was when the naysayers began: "People like you don't get married—who do you think you are?" "Why get married and ruin a good thing?" "You think you're too good for the rest of us." Hurtful words brought about hurtful reactions, and soon arguments started, and the wedding plans fell apart. She left Michigan for California, and he was left holding a broken heart.

He was telling me this story at the St. Vincent de Paul shop where he had come for help, trying to put his life back together.

"That's really sad," I sympathized.

He shook his head and smiled. "It's going to be all right. We stopped praying—that's what happened. Once we had received all that we prayed for, we forgot where it came from. We won't make that mistake again. My fiancée and I are praying again. God will take care of the rest."

"Are you still engaged?"

"No." He smiled shyly. "But we will be soon. First, we have to pray her back from California. And this time, when she comes back, we won't stop praying."

"And the naysayers?"

"Funny, that. When my fiancée left, everyone wanted to come over to my place and hang out. It was as if my unhappiness made them happy. They aren't welcome in my home anymore. But God is. I won't ever stop praying again."

"Don't ever stop praying" felt like a message from God to me. But how to do it better? I went back to the idea of the family prayer list. Maybe I should start writing things down again and be more intentional about it. I picked up Aunt Kay's rosary and gazed at the amethyst beads. *Fifty Hail Mary beads.* Hmm . . . ?

I went to a bookshelf, found a pad of paper, and sat down in my prayer place. Using a pen, I wrote the numbers one through fifty in two columns. With the rosary clasped between my fingers, I closed my eyes and began to pray. As I prayed, my worries fought for my attention over the words of the prayers and the mysteries of the rosary I was trying to meditate on. Honestly, lately my worries had been so intrusive it felt as if I hadn't even prayed.

But this time, when someone's name came to mind or some problem crowded out peacefulness, I wrote it down on the list next to a number. The physical act of writing the names and problems began to free up my mind a tiny bit.

The names came faster and faster. I was writing people and worries on the pad of paper for the entire twenty minutes that it took to say the prayers. By the time I finished with "Hail, Holy Queen," I had filled the page. It felt good. I was calm. I had lifted them each in prayer. My loved ones were out of the mucky floodwaters and sitting in the truck with Jesus.

I prayed with that list on my lap each day for the entire month. Some of the petitions were answered, but I didn't cross them out. I kept naming them, this time with a "thank you" included. A petition might change from "Please, help Caroline's pregnancy progress smoothly" to "Thank you, Lord, that mom and baby are doing well," or "May his soul rest in peace." During the thirty days, other names would come to me while I prayed, and I would assign them to one of the Our Father or Glory Be beads, and that way I wasn't locked into only the original fifty.

On the first day of the following month, I turned the page over in the notebook and listed one through fifty again—fresh and empty. I closed my eyes and prayed, and names came to me; some new, some from the old list, and some people who didn't even seem to need prayers. I didn't argue. If their name came to mind while I was praying, then who was I to choose who needed prayer or who didn't? Of course, most of my family members were on the list and many friends. The pope, world leaders, and neighbors appeared. Whole groups of people in war zones, hurricanes, and earthquakes found their places. I could do it in twenty minutes, the list transformed every month, and no one was ever scratched out. It had the effect that St. Vincent advocated when he said, "Free your mind from all that troubles you; God will take care of things."

It was a family prayer list I could love.

If one through fifty feels like a burden, try one through twenty-five. Prayer should lift us up out of the mire of worry. Giving our concerns to God is meant to be a daily release from troubles, so don't make it into work: "just keep praying."

11

Four Muslim Families

Judaism, Christianity, and Islam all worship the God of Abraham. While writing this book, a unique opportunity came to me to find out how Muslims pray in their families to the God that we all love. The Muslim people regularly show up on my prayer list because I hear so often about wars occurring in countries in which that faith is prominent. I felt entirely blessed to be welcomed by Muslim families and to be entrusted to share these very personal prayer stories. I pray that everyone who reads their stories receives a blessing, too.

A Time to Pray

On a cold February day, Dean and I drive to Indianapolis to meet four Muslim families who have volunteered to talk to us about family prayer. Their children all attend the same Islamic school. The third-grade teacher is the daughter of longtime friends, which is how we were given this opportunity. I am nervous about this because I have only a basic understanding of Islam, and these people are strangers, and everyone is aware of the tensions in the world. But these families have agreed to be interviewed by a Catholic author about prayer, and they are likely a million times more nervous than I am, so Dean and I pray together on the four-hour drive and leave it in God's hands.

We arrive in town near the end of the school day. The principal, Dr. Rashid, welcomes us into his office and, between teachers and students popping in and out with questions, he introduces us to the five basic pillars of Islam, the practices that all Muslims do, one of which is praying five times each day. I take notes, but I explain to him that this book is not going to be long enough to describe Islam in even an outline form, and that what I am really interested in are stories about how Muslim families pray together. Dr. Rashid listens, and then says humbly, "In my family, I struggle. I am not only the principal of this school but also the imam at the mosque. My kids don't want to pray with me because I take too long. In the morning, we pray before sunrise, and I don't want to wait for them to get up because I don't want to miss prayer time. My wife says I am too impatient."

I tell him that I often hear similar confessions from my Christian friends: "The rosary is too long for kids," or "I can't get them up in time for church." Dean and I nod and commiserate, admitting our own struggles, and soon we are all more at ease. Dr. Rashid's daughter flies through the office door looking for her boots that are tumbled in front of his desk. She snatches them up, chatters to her dad about an upcoming test, and dashes back into the hallway. He smiles fondly after her and says, "We teach children to pray between the ages of seven to ten, and after that they are responsible to pray on their own initiative. Prayer in the home is good, of course, but prayer at the mosque is encouraged more. Community is important, and praying at specific times during the day is key. When we are praying, we know that all the Muslims in our community are praying at the same time." He pauses. "In some families, they have set aside a room for prayer. That is wonderful if it can be done. My family prays on special rugs, but perhaps you will meet someone today who has a more specific place in their home."

This possibility intrigues me. I have a corner in my living room where I pray each morning, but the space is not obvious nor is it used only for prayer. It just happens to be where I pray. The concept of having a place set aside within the home for talking with God seems like a wonderful dream.

A Place to Pray

The next family we meet has invited us to come to their home. Dr. and Mrs. Alshami (not his real name) have three young daughters and originally came to the United States from Damascus, Syria. He went to medical school in Detroit, has a practice in internal medicine in Indianapolis, and his wife, Deena, is a dentist. Their nearly new home is located in a popular subdivision close to the school. They listen carefully as I explain my interest in how their family prays together. He tells us about praying at the mosque on Friday evenings and talks about the profound importance of fasting during Ramadan. I take notes and try to ask again about how they pray at home. The couple exchanges pensive looks and speaks quietly together in Arabic. I get the feeling that I am probing into something personal.

After consulting Deena, Dr. Alshami stands and invites us to see their prayer room. We follow them into the kitchen, past the dining table, and into a lovely sitting area with large windows on three sides. The furniture is modern and comfortable; light and warmth come from all directions. Shy Deena glows when she sees our admiration of the room, and she tells us the story behind its creation.

"Our eldest daughter, Hala, was interested in prayer from the time she was one and a half years old. She was so happy when we took her to the mosque with us, and everyone there was delighted to see her. When she was about five years old, she wanted to learn to pray. She was quite young, but we saw that she was serious, so we began to teach her at home. She soon let us know that she didn't like to pray in the same room with the television or with toys. She chose to go into the office to pray instead because there were fewer distractions. She even renamed it and began calling it 'the house of Allah.'" Deena smiles at the memory. "In 2015, we decided to build this house. Hala was excited and looked at the plans with us. She asked, 'Where will the house of Allah be in our new home? It has to be the most beautiful room in the house!' We had not expected her to be so fervent, but she insisted. So, we consulted with the builder, and we added this room to the plans."

Dr. Alshami then chuckles and says, "If we pray on a rug, it is easy to change the direction so that we are praying toward Mecca, but a room is not so simple. When we asked the builder to change the orientation of the house on the lot for a better view, this room faced exactly northeast, which is the direction Muslims pray in the United States."

They show us the glass cabinet in the corner that holds the Quran and a prayer sculpture that has the ninety-nine names of Allah engraved on it. When their daughters pray, the girls put on prayer smocks that their mom has sewn by hand, and these are kept close by in the house of Allah, too. Dean and I admire the special garments, and the young mother continues in her soft voice, "Hala tells me, 'I feel happy when I go to pray.' And sometimes, when we are stressed," she says, alluding to the catastrophe that is taking place in Syria, "we all pray here together. It's a way to comfort us."

A Reason to Pray

Farheen, a young mother from Pakistan, leans forward over the table between us. We are at the mosque, and she has to pick up her kids from school soon, so she speaks quickly and intensely. It is a challenge to write fast enough to keep up with her.

"In my home country, we speak Urdu, not Arabic, so when I recited the suras (verses from the Quran), I didn't know what I was saying. When the community prayed, I prayed, when they fasted, I fasted. I just did what my parents did, but I had no deep understanding of anything." Her face lights up. "When I came here in 2005, people asked me questions about Islam that I couldn't answer. I began experiencing my faith in a different way. I began studying Arabic so that I could teach my children. It was embarrassing when they asked me questions from their schoolwork about Islam and I didn't know the answers. Now when I teach my children the prayers and the suras, I also translate them, and they are confident when they ask me. But I am still at a medium level—Arabic is like an ocean!"

I ask Farheen if she has a story about teaching her children about prayer. She thinks a moment, then says: "My daughter Suphia came to me and said, 'I really need a bike! My friend has a new bike and it is pink and shiny and,' on and on. She had just turned seven, and this is when she was first learning about prayer, so I said to her, 'Did you say your prayers today?' She answered no. I said, 'Did you know that after you say your prayers you can ask Allah for a bike? You can ask him anything you like.' She was so excited. The next prayer time, I was not there to remind her, but she did it all by herself. When I came inside the house, I saw her doing it with big gestures and speaking loudly. We did buy her the bike, and after that she stopped begging for things. If I said no, she was fine; she just asked Allah instead. Suphia had complete faith in prayer. This lasted about two weeks, then she slowed down a bit, but she is still doing her prayers."

Farheen smiles broadly. "It changed her for a few weeks, but it changed me more. It made me reflect on how well I was doing the prayers. Now, every single time I tell my kids to do something, I reflect on how well *I am doing it*. I am answerable in front of Allah in how I act. I don't feel like an adult in front of Allah; I feel like a child because I feel like I am expected to behave. Also, I am expecting my kids to obey Allah, not obey just me. I also have boundaries, as they do."

"This is a very good thing, raising our kids here. They don't see the community celebrating, fasting, and so on, so that is my responsibility to show them. The good thing about coming here is I'm a better Muslim here."

Children to Pray With

Houari Dahmani came to the United States from Algeria. He and his wife, an architect, have three young children, ages three to eleven. He is a computer specialist and spends his free time as a soccer coach for young people. We meet at a coffee shop near a busy highway, and I ask him about family prayer.

"The teaching of prayer usually goes from parent to child, but I did not learn that way because, when I was young, my father did not pray. His father did not pray either. I began to pray at about age eleven because of the people in our town. I had an older friend who asked me to go to the mosque with him. When I developed an interest in praying, the benefits increased. It was after I started that my father began to pray, too."

"I am not making the same mistake with my children, so my kids see my wife or me praying. Actually, I pray with my kids more than with my wife. On Fridays, I take them to the mosque, but I don't need to push them. I teach myself and my kids to try always to pray on time because Allah prescribed that we do it on time, five times each day. We have rugs everywhere in the house so that whenever it is time for prayer, we get ready, we pray, and we connect with him. When I got married, I told Allah that if he gave me a child, I would take him to the mosque. He gave me three!"

Houari smiles with the joy of this great gift. "The story goes that when the Prophet Muhammad prayed and he touched his head to the floor, his young children would climb on his back, but he never brushed them off. My littlest son does the same to me, and I don't brush him off, either."

I imagine this young, athletic, soccer-coach father honoring Allah by kneeling, head to the carpet, with his small children climbing on his back and joining him in the joy of such a prayer.

Many religions advise praying at regular times. The Liturgy of the Hours prayed by some Christians is a good example. My cousin Mary Kay and her husband, Jim, try to attend Mass on the first Saturday of each month out of respect for the Blessed Virgin Mary. I do my best to pray the Divine Mercy Chaplet at 3:00 p.m., the hour Jesus died on the cross. And sunrise and sunset are typical times of prayer in many faith practices.

Do you pray at a specific time? For a week, on your prayer list write the time of day that you pray. You could ask God if he prefers to make your time with him more regular. Maybe he's fine with the way it is.

12

Praying Like Children

My children, my nieces and nephews, and my friends' children take up large swaths of my prayer list, as do old people. They are the vulnerable ones in my life, or at least, they appear to be. But after several months of collecting family prayer stories, I began to be persuaded that children pray so innocently and so purely that God must be putty in their little folded hands. Maybe, along with them being on my prayer list, what I need to do is make sure that I am on theirs!

This first story is written by my friend Julie Pequignot Nolan. I met her in 2012, when she invited me to speak at her parish in Indiana. Julie is a school-bus driver, and her love of children abounds. She also knows how to tell a story.

At Grandmother's Grandmother's Table

We are blessed to have our grandchildren visit often, and mealtime is especially beautiful, as our little ones share so much wisdom with us. We sit at a small kitchen table that belonged to my grandmother, the most prayerful person I've ever known. We could move into the dining room, but we don't. This small table is perfect for close conversations, elbow-to-elbow manners, and, even as our little brood grows, this is the best spot to witness life.

After the Catholic meal prayer, Bless Us, O Lord, we go around the table offering up intentions. When they are small toddlers, they most likely pray for "Mommy" or "Daddy" or with a little smirk on their face, "I'll pray for you, MawMaw or PawPaw." As they grow, they pray for classmates, deceased relatives, pets, swing sets, good grades . . . the list goes on and on.

For nearly two years, at least one of them prayed weekly for Sunshine, my cat that had run away: "Watch over Sunshine." "Bring Sunshine back." "I hope Sunshine finds her family." "I miss Sunshine." This weekly prayer request always brought a grimace to my face, until finally I said, "No more praying for Sunshine!" Stunned faces whipped in my direction. "Well, I think we need to use our intentions on something different after all this time."

The real truth is that MawMaw had accidently run over Sunshine two years before. I'd raced her to the veterinarian and had a costly conversation about reconstruction and the value of life for an injured cat and, with the advice of our vet, put her down. My remorse was enormous, and week after week *for two years* they turned the dagger in my guilt-ridden heart with their sweet prayers. My secret is safe with you, right?

There are five of them now, and they shout out, "I'm first!" the minute they sit down to the table, and the prayers start flying up to Our Lord. My husband is always the last to go, and he prays for his grandchildren. Often this solicits a "PawPaw, can't you pray for anything else?" But he never does; he knows where our prayers are needed most.

"And a Child Shall Lead Them . . ."

The Gibbs family, from Canton, Ohio, had a long tradition of saying grace before meals, and the adults included the children as soon as they were old enough to learn the words. Little Frederick was a preschooler when this story took place.

It was Thanksgiving, and the entire clan had gathered around the dining room table for the feast. The turkey was centered on the white tablecloth, the cranberry sauce beside it. Mounds of potatoes and green beans, stuffing and yams, steamed in the serving bowls. Everyone sat down, and Grandpa bowed his head, sending the signal that it was time to pray. He looked up in the silence and spotted the littlest member of the clan, sitting eagerly forward in his chair. "Frederick," Grandpa said, "would you please offer the prayer?"

The little guy's eyes opened in panic, but his mother leaned close and whispered the beginning line that he knew well. "God is great . . ."

Frederick's face calmed, and he spoke out confidently, "God is great, God is good. And his fleece is white as snow."

When I visited my sister-in-law Kim, she told me this story about praying at home as a child.

Joe's Grace

When I was small, my mom used to sit with me at night and teach me to pray and listen to my prayers. Later, during my teenage years, she would come to me and ask me to pray for situations. I asked her why she wanted my prayers, and she said, "Because your prayers always come true." I don't know why she said that.

Anyway, we said bedtime prayers but never said a table grace. No one in our extended family did, either. I don't know if there was a reason for this; it was just the way we did things. When my youngest brother, Joe, was three or four, out of the blue he decided that it was something we should do. "We need to say prayers before we eat," he would pester before every meal.

Eventually, when he wouldn't let it go, my mom said, "Okay. What do you want to say?"

Joe folded his hands and said, "Thank you for our food. Amen."

That became our family tradition, and we said Joe's grace at every meal. Even now, if someone asks me to lead grace, that's what I say.

Praying on Their Own

When Ellen and Martha were about five and six, they often played with some neighbor children who lived a block away. Our street doesn't have sidewalks, so I would always walk with them to be sure they arrived safely. One day, Louise, the children's mom, called to ask if our girls could come over.

"I just put muffins in the oven, so I can't leave," I told her.

"Send them, and I'll wait in front of my house. No worries—I'll watch them the whole way." We lived on a dead-end street, so the risk was slight.

That sounded like a good plan, and they needed to start learning how to walk around by themselves a little, so I instructed them to hold hands, and I walked them to the street. We could see Louise waving her arm, and they started off. Then I went back in the house to give them confidence in their own abilities.

A few minutes later, Louise called me on the phone, laughing. "You can sure tell who are the little Catholic kids on the block," she said (Louise is a good Baptist).

I had a funny feeling about that statement. "Umm . . . you can? So, what's up?"

"Your girls were so cute, walking hand in hand and all. They were almost here, but suddenly they stopped. At first, I couldn't tell what was going on, but then I remembered that there was a dead crow on the side of the road. I thought, *Oh, crimey—are they going to start crying?* but they didn't. They talked it over a little bit, then they both knelt down on the side of the road, folded their hands, and said a prayer. It was adorable, but I nearly died trying not to laugh."

I chuckled, too, but I was sincerely pleased that my little daughters knew how to cope when tragedy struck.

Amen!

When my nephew Phil was a toddler, only beginning to talk, he had a vocabulary of about thirty words. They included the usual *B* words like *baby, ball, bye-bye, brrr, big,* and *bottle.* He could name Mama, Dada, and Santa, but most of his communication was done with pointing fingers, grunts, and squeals—ordinary baby stuff.

From the beginning of their marriage, before each meal, his parents clasped hands and said grace, so Phil regularly heard the rhythmical cadence of "Bless us, O Lord, and these thy gifts which we are about to receive from thy bounty, through Christ our Lord. Amen." But of course, he wasn't old enough to pray along with them.

One day, Phil crawled over to his highchair and pulled himself upright. He looked across the room at his mom and said plainly, "Amen."

"Amen?" she said, startled that he even knew that word and confused about what he meant by saying it to her so directly.

"Amen! Amen! Amen!" he insisted, shaking the legs of the chair. "Amen!"

She cocked her head at him. "Are you hungry, Phil?" she asked.

"Amen!" He nodded happily and clapped his hands.

Try to remember what it felt like to pray as a child. On your prayer list, it might be nice to have a brief prayer at the top. Some months, I write a Scripture verse or a prayer from my devotional reading. Or you could write something spontaneous and simple, like what a child might say. Use short sentences and small words.

13

Reading Scripture as Family Prayer

Becky and I have known each other since our kids were tiny. She and Brian lived across the street, and we always celebrated Halloween together; she and I handed out candy at home while Dean and Brian escorted the costumed offspring to all the neighbors' porches. After everyone was cold and tired, we gathered in front of our fireplace and sipped hot cider. Did we pray together? Not that I recall.

But now that we are older and our children are no longer children, we do pray together. Becky, me, and another friend, Bonnie, get together every two months to share lunch and pray for our grown children. It's a family prayer list that encompasses three families. Here is Becky's story of family prayer.

In my husband Brian's family, they read from the Bible every night after dinner, along with a corresponding message from a small monthly publication such as *The Upper Room* or *Our Daily Bread*. This practice went back to his great-grandparents' era.

When Brian and I married, I was just over the threshold of being a new believer in Christ, and this Bible-reading custom seemed stuffy and old-fashioned to me. He insisted that it was important, though, so we continued. Gradually as my faith grew, this pattern began to cement itself comfortably in my heart. I say "cement," because it implies something that is fixed in a position of permanence. Neither of us fully understood in our younger years that, although tradition has value, some flexibility is vital for preserving things. In the meantime, we looked forward to our future family sitting around the table sharing in this ritual.

Brian and I had a daughter and then, five years later, a son. We continued reading the Bible after dinner. Both children began to take turns with the reading when they could sound out words. I'd like to describe the gladness and reverence that colored these times, when the children sat with their hands folded, listening with round eyes, eager to hear every word and make saintly comments that we could quote in our Christmas letter to relatives, if we wrote one.

Not so much.

Small children have small attention spans. When the "Amen" part came around, it might have been sandwiched between reverent gems like, "Stop poking me!" or "She didn't close her eyes when we prayed!" Or "God spelled backwards is *dog*."

One night, our daughter seemed introspective. At the end of the passage, she looked up hesitantly and said, "I have a question."

"Of course, honey," I prompted. "You can ask Dad and me anything, and we'll try to answer it as best as we can."

"Okay. Do you think I'd look good with bangs, or should I keep growing my hair out?"

Resistance to this tradition ebbed and flowed. Upon reaching the teenage years, our kids felt self-conscious about doing the readings when their friends joined us for dinner, and they wanted to skip this family practice. We still read, though, and sometimes a friend of theirs wanted to take a turn reading. Possibly, those were among the few times these kids ever read God's word. By now, my husband and I were learning some things about flexibility and the importance of trying to show how Scripture was relevant to the kids' lives. Some-times, the Bible verses sparked great discussion. Or it might lead to laughing over odd customs or a strange-sounding biblical name such as Methuselah. Other times, there might be awkward silence, as the message hit home with unwelcomed conviction. And it wasn't always just the kids who were silent. Ouch!

Our children are now adults and creating their own traditions. Last Christmas after dinner, I read from a commentary that Brian's dad had saved several years before he passed away, about our greatest need being God. God wants us to want him. Something has to click and become personal; otherwise it's just a mechanical action, a tradition without meaning.

> *As the deer pants for streams of water,*
> *so my soul pants for you, my God.*
>
> —Psalm 42:1

God's word gets out—awkward silence or not.

✎ **Would this be a good time to open Scripture and add a verse to your prayer list?**

14

Holy Water, Candles, Eggs, Coffee, and Linen

For more than twenty-five years, Dean and I were part of a team that led weekend retreats for couples in our diocese preparing for the sacrament of marriage. For most of that time, Joe Schmitt was the diocesan director of the Office of Marriage and Family Ministry. We spent long weekends together sharing with young people about the role of God in our marriage, which, of course, included prayer. Joe is a major part of the reason that Dean and I feel comfortable praying together.

In recent years, Joe left his job and studied to become an ordained deacon. Now, he baptizes, witnesses marriage vows, preaches from the pulpit, visits hospital beds, and still finds time to counsel young couples who are launching a life together. I asked him if he would share some wisdom over a cup of coffee, and the following came from that conversation.

Holy Water

"I can't separate life from prayer anymore. It's all mixed together. That's why it's good to get people involved in the church celebrations—get their hands in the mud, so to speak," Joe tells me. "When a family comes to church to get a baby baptized, I turn it into a family prayer. During the baptismal rite, you know how we recite the litany of saints, naming all those people who died centuries ago? It's good to do that, and then I ask, 'What saints have preceded us in *this* family?' People start calling out names of grandparents, great-grands, aunts and uncles, and anyone in the family who has died."

He smiles: "After that, there is a part of the rite where the minister prays that the Holy Spirit will come down into the baptismal water. I ask all the little kids to surround the font, and I tell them, 'I need your help; this water needs to move to make sure the Holy Spirit is mixed well into it.' They put their little hands into the basin and swish it all around while I am invoking the Spirit, and they become part of the prayer. Then I tell the parents to take some of the water home and bless their kids with it as often as possible."

"When I was first ordained and we would travel back home for family reunions, my dad's cousin Verda would always ask me for a blessing. She was nearly ninety years old, the matriarch, and it made me uncomfortable to be put in this role. My wife, Becky, would elbow me and whisper, 'She really wants it, Joe. Just do it,' so I put my unease aside and gave her a blessing. Eventually, I realized that Verda wasn't asking for *my* blessing; she wanted *Jesus'* blessing that flows through ordination."

I ask Joe, "How do you bless Verda now?"

"I say, 'Lord, this woman is asking for your blessing. She is your servant here on earth, and she blesses all of us in many ways as we mingle on our journey. We ask this blessing in your name, Father, Son, and Holy Spirit.' Then I like to trace the brand that she has on her forehead from her baptism—the one we all have. It's important to go over that cross. Parents should do it every night when they put the kids to bed. It reminds the child of their baptism, and it reminds the parents of their commitment to help each other see Christ in everyone."

Candles

Dean and I, being an ecumenical couple, have four feet to stand on in both the Lutheran and Catholic denominations. We attend both Mass and Sunday services, potlucks and fish fries, Sunday school and faith formation, sing with guitars or organs, buy raffle tickets, and bake casseroles by the dozens. The cultural parts of church congregations can be difficult to distinguish from the doctrines. But when the candles, paraments, vestments, hymns, statues, windows, pews, painted ceilings, water fonts, and the language of church draw us in with their beauty, we can find God there.

I am a guest speaker at both Catholic and Protestant churches. When the question-and-answer part of the talk feels comfortable, I am asked by my Protestant brothers and sisters to explain some Catholic practices that seem odd to them. Recently, a lady shyly asked me why Catholics light candles with such abandon. This question brought a smile to my face—I'm one of those happy candle lighters.

Many Catholic parishes have shrines scattered about their sanctuaries, where votive candles are available to light. People with family or private intentions such as illness, loss, or unfulfilled hopes, set a little flame burning to remind them of the constant action of prayer. As children, our daughters would often ask to light a candle at church, especially if they were worried about someone who was ill. They paid for them with coins slipped into a box and loved adding to the racks of flaming prayers.

I also light prayer candles at home. Why limit myself to birthday cakes, citronella, or mood lighting? My family counts the weeks before Christmas with an Advent wreath of three purple candles and a pink one. When the children were small, they took very seriously the responsibility of burning a new candle each week in anticipation of their favorite day of the year.

On Candlemas Day, in the dead of winter, when the priest blesses all the church candles for the coming year, I tote a sack of my own to church to have them sprinkled with holy water and prayed over. These are my morning prayer candles that I light when the house is still dark, the prayer list is in my lap, and no one but me and God are up. We talk the day over and watch the eastern sky turn pink and orange while the candle flickers and reminds me that even a tiny flame is enough to wake me up and make me feel warmer. Striking the match is the beginning of daily prayer, and watching the small flame centers my attention on God.

Eggs

During Lent, my family uses candles to pray in a different way. We make Ukrainian Easter eggs called *pysanky*, using a wax-release method of decorating. The wax is melted in a tiny brass funnel (a *kistka*) and applied to the eggshell to form intricate designs and layered colors. To melt the wax, we hold the *kistka* over a candle flame, usually a leftover candle from our Advent wreath. It requires a steady hand, patience, and slow, fine movements to decorate eggs this way. It also requires prayer. We always begin with the sign of the cross and the whispered words, "God, help me."

It can take several hours to decorate one egg, and the time is spent in quiet conversation or meditation as my eyes become nearsighted and background distractions fade. *Pysanky* are meant to be gifts presented to loved ones on Easter morning—no bunnies bring these lovely creations. While writing in wax on the fragile eggshells, I try to keep in mind the needs and desires of the person who will receive the gift. The hours in front of the candle turn into a joyful and personal way to pray for people, and the egg transforms into a tiny, personal prayer list.

John Grap and his wife, Linda, are another couple living Christian unity in their everyday lives, even while their churches stay separated. I was introduced to John through a fellow author, and he told me this story.

Coffee as Prayer

Linda and I have been married thirty-four years. She is Methodist, and I am Catholic, but we have both tried different practices over the years—from dropping out, to becoming evangelical born-again, to both of us practicing as Methodist, to circling back to where we are now. We don't do the kind of praying on our knees that we used to do years ago. Our prayer time has evolved into something as simple as me bringing her coffee in the morning. It's not only a secret to a good marriage; it's also an act of prayer.

I'm not sure what type of prayer matters to God. Is it prayer that acknowledges him and expresses our love? That's what I'm doing when I bring my wife coffee.

To round out this chapter about praying with ordinary things, I return to my conversation with Deacon Joe Schmitt. He comes from a large extended clan, one of eleven siblings. I asked him if he had any stories about family prayer in a mobile world in which families are often separated by continents and oceans.

Table Linen

"My oldest sister, Pat, has been the family hostess for Thanksgiving since my parents passed away," Joe reminisces. "For thirty-five years she has used the same white linen tablecloth that covers a table for fifteen or more people. Along with the silverware and plates, Pat provides permanent colored markers for her guests. At prayer time, everyone writes directly on the linen the thing that they are most grateful for that year. New babies and new homes, jobs, diplomas, vacations, healing, and love—it all gets printed carefully on the cloth. The inscriptions are signed and dated, too."

"As I read the notes around my plate each year, I see the signatures of relatives who passed away, and it feels as if they are still at the table with us. Usually the phone rings several times during dinner, and family members who aren't able to travel to be with us call in their notations of thanks to be added to the collection. The last time I was there, they were writing small and tucking the gratitude along the hem because the cloth was so plastered with decades of thanks. It's a wonderful way to spread prayer out over the years."

My prayer list is not all about petitions. Sometimes my heart wells up with gratitude. I put new babies on my list, newly earned diplomas, and engaged couples. I also include trees, flowers, and wild creatures on the list from time to time.

Do you sometimes pray with an object? A candle? A set of beads? Water? Coffee? Today, fetch that object and set it in front of you as you pray, thanking God for his "blessings without number and mercies without end" (from the hymn "O God, Beyond All Praising") that are the myriad of ordinary things that make up our world.

15

Singing Prayers

In the midst of our struggles, Dean and I kept praying, but one of the things that became difficult was singing. His cough and shortness of breath took the fun out of that activity. Since we bought our house, there was always a piano in the living room. Dean played for the fun of it. He was also an occasional substitute organist at church, and he sang in several choirs over the years. But through three years of downward-spiraling health, we didn't even sing many Christmas carols together.

During this time, I met a ten-year-old girl who was humming "Silent Night." This is how our conversation went.

He Needs It

Ten-year-old girl is humming.

Me: That's my favorite carol.

Girl: Do you like music?

Me: Yes, I do. Do you like it?

Girl: I sing a lot.

Me: Do you sing all day long?

Girl: Sometimes.

Me: Even when you're sad?

Girl: Yes, that's when I sing the most.

Her answer made me pause what I was doing and look at her more closely. It was a moment in which I became aware that God's presence depended on my willingness to be fully present, too.

Me: What do you sing?

Girl: I sing to Jesus. He needs it.

Me: Ah, you're right. He does need it.

Girl: Yeah.

Jesus had made this little girl into a messenger to me, but I needed to listen to her soft humming to notice it. Sometimes God speaks to me through my own prayers or through listening closely to others' prayers.

He speaks to me if I take time to listen to the children.

Shortly after I met this precious girl, our daughter Martha quit her job overseas and returned to Michigan (one prayer answered), and two weeks later, Dean landed in the emergency room with congestive heart failure caused by a defective mitral valve (more prayers needed!). Martha is a medical librarian, and it was absolutely crucial to have her by my side while I tried to navigate the medical system and comprehend what the doctors were trying to explain to us.

Dean needed major surgery, and he needed it in a hurry.

Martha and her sister, Ellen, were with us for the entire two weeks in the hospital. They took on the enormous task of communication between us and family and friends. They made the phone calls to family, posted the e-mail updates and the Facebook requests for prayers, and they taught me how to send texts on my track phone from the

ICU. Most of those messages involved prayer. I am forever grateful that we already knew how to pray together.

And I became aware of how singing is a comforting way to pray under pressure.

Will and Bess are our longtime friends. They practice an original type of American music called shape note, or sacred harp. In the long hospital days when Dean was awaiting surgery, fighting to breathe and struggling to catch mere moments of sleep, our friends prayed with their Mennonite congregation. They also came to the hospital and sat with me in the waiting room. And—the best gift of all—they sang to Dean. They visited briefly in his dimly lit hospital room and chose slow, peaceful tunes to help him relax and find a rhythm to breathe in.

When the ordeal was over, after Dean recovered enough to attend a shape note gathering, he chose the following hymn to lead:

#475 "A Thankful Heart"

Give me a calm, a thankful heart from every murmur free;
The blessing of thy grace impart and make me live to thee.

What is your favorite hymn? From memory, try to write a few of the lines. Look at the names on your prayer list and sing or hum the hymn for the people there. This is another way to pray.

16

Praying in a Crisis

After Dean's seven hours of surgery, he spent some days in the ICU with nineteen wires and tubes sticking out of him. Over that time, the nurses transitioned him from flat on his back and breathing on a respirator to walking with three helpers assisting, to eating a normal diet. Finally, after three days, they let him have his cell phone back.

While he was in the ICU and could receive only one visitor at a time, we took turns sitting near his bed and texting his progress to other family members in the waiting room. I had not texted much before this, but with our daughters' help, I learned quickly. Many of our texts were requests for prayer and "allcluias" when those prayers were answered. A new advantage of praying this way is that photos can be included. I could take a picture of Dean and type: "Look! He's off oxygen! God is good," and everyone could respond with shared joy and encouragement.

One of the people who supported me during this crisis was my dear friend Brenda. I phoned her when things were at their worst, and, from then on, we kept in touch by texts. Nowadays, we see each other about every six months for intense sharing, but especially we ponder the things God seems to be doing in our lives. Between these heart-to-heart conversations, the only way to know what is going on with her and her family is to begin with a few emoji and follow it up with: "Is this a good time?"

If it is, indeed, a good time, we text back and forth long strings of catching up and affection.

During one of these "conversations," we were typing about the difficulty of praying with family when the members are spread out all over the country. I asked Brenda how her family prays with one another. Her response:

> "Oh my! I know! . . . you have me thinking! Actually, we text our prayers a lot. We now have this family prayer journal of sorts. . . . We can go back and see how our relationships have grown stronger since we've been doing this and how some things that made us so angry or frustrated or scared are no longer there, that God has answered our prayers in one way or another. It really has grown because at first it was more about people we knew who were sick or who were going into surgery. . . . Now we pray for all sorts of big and small things, anytime!"

I asked her if she would be comfortable sharing some of her family prayer texts, and she was fine with that. For background, Brenda's daughter Laurel is in the middle of a general surgery residency at a busy hospital in Chicago. The text conversation that follows is between Brenda and her three sisters, Mimi, Nancy, and Linda.

Texting the Family Prayer List

Tues., Sept. 26, 2:01 p.m.

Brenda

Hi guys! Can you please pray a little special prayer for Laurel?

She just got off of a 24 hour shift and was in the OR from 9 AM til 7:30 a.m. She never sat down for 24 hours. Ate a protein bar and a bagel. And drank coffee. And someone stole her Lululemon jacket from the hooks outside the OR. $120 zip-up. Her favorite. Then she accidently got in the front seat with the Uber driver! She's exhausted. I pray she gets rested and they find her jacket. Cuz I prayed to St. Anthony and it would be so cool for God to get glorified! Or that we can forgive that person and not be angry in our hearts toward them. I pray she can have a happy, restored attitude. That she sees His face in a patient or a coworker.

Mimi

On our way to Bible study. Will get everyone to pray there, too!

Brenda

Thank you so much!

Nancy

Yes! At the airport. Flying home. Had a great time. Will pray on the way!

Brenda

Thank you, Nancy!!! Looks like you had a fantastic time! 🖤

Nancy

Yes. Boarding now!

Linda

Will pray for her. For peace and confidence. I know she is stressed but this will truly make her stronger for having accomplished such incredible feats as she has during this.

Brenda

Me too! Thanks! 🖤 😊

Brenda

Please pray for Mike's sweet Nona. (Mike is Laurel's fiancé.) She is the one who turned 100. We think she is dying. Pray for a gentle passing and that she is welcomed into Jesus' loving arms. She has a special love for Mary. Pictures of Mary are everywhere in her place. Mike's mom is trying to get to Chicago. She is sick from her chemo treatment. 😞

Mimi

I will pray! We are in the Basilica of the Sacred Heart at Notre Dame. Just finished Mass.

Will say a prayer before we leave.

Brenda

Oh my!! I love this. Beautiful!

Nancy

Praying for Nona! Mimi, beautiful altar! Love that place. Imagine she'll see God and his Throne in heaven! He is calling her. Soon all her pain will be done. Joy and everlasting Peace.

Brenda: From Laurel

Wonderful! Tell everyone thanks. What beautiful things for them all to say—I'll pass on the message. I wish I could go visit (Mike's Nona)—I'm at work. I'll go tomorrow if she doesn't pass before then.

I asked Brenda how she felt about praying by typing on her phone, and she said, "I think, for my daughter, it helps soften the blow. With her job as a surgeon, she is often exhausted and frustrated, but she has these aunts who are loving her through a string of texts right in the moment when she needs it most."

"It wasn't about the Lululemon jacket. She never saw that coat again. Prayer is about God's love lifting us up. The text-praying gives me and my sisters strength. I tell my friends how I pray with my family this way, and sometimes I hear from loved ones who don't pray, who text me, 'Would you get your sisters to pray for me?'"

"It takes time to grow and get comfortable praying with people. Texting is a beginning. Texting can be a way to pray for family members who aren't yet comfortable."

Texting is so immediate and so everyday that it opens family prayer to be that way, too. Ever since Dean's time in the ICU, I have used texting to pray with my family.

The next story is from a relative of a relative—not my kin but my kith. She has a great devotion to St. Joseph, spouse of the Virgin Mary and a favorite saint of many people in the Catholic Church. Joseph is known as the patron of married couples, families, fathers, laborers (especially carpenters), home sellers (he and Mary moved a few times), the Universal Church, and a happy death. Catholics do not pray to saints as if they were God—we know there is only one God. Rather, we ask the saints to pray for us just as we ask our friends and family to pray for us. The Communion of Saints is a real, active community that resides both on earth and in heaven, and all of them can be called upon to pray for us in any type of trouble.

St. Joseph had a lot to deal with in his life. His fiancée became pregnant before they were together, but he married her anyway. The baby was born while they were traveling; then Joseph had to keep Mary and Jesus safe from a murderous king, and, finally, they fled their homeland and became refugees. It's easy to see why he is the patron saint of families! The following is a story of how, through a family's petitions, St. Joseph prayed for another baby to be safe in a deadly crisis.

St. Joseph in a Crisis

This is a story that began in my childhood. St. Joseph has been my friend and mentor, and I have dearly loved him since I was five years old, and he has been my father figure since I lost my biological father at age three. Joseph, being a regular human who found himself in an extraordinary circumstance, was someone I could relate to all my life. My devotion to St. Joseph is a private prayer that is meant to teach my children to pray by themselves whenever they need his help.

I have found that he never fails to answer my prayers no matter how serious my problem is, and I think my children have discovered he always responds with sympathy and empathy. He is my hero and has never failed me.

Here is just one example of many.

When I was pregnant with my son Joseph (yes, he is named for St. Joseph), my daughter Leah and son Jack came down with the German measles—*and so did I.* My pediatrician, my primary-care physician, and second-opinion doctors all urged me to abort. They even privately called in my husband, Jeff, to persuade him to urge me to abort. That was unthinkable to my husband and me. We had tried for two years to conceive this precious baby.

I talked and talked to St. Joseph and asked Leah, Jack, and Jeff to talk to him. We all petitioned for St. Joseph's prayers alone, not together. Talking to St. Joseph has always been a very private thing for me. The result: I gave birth to a beautiful, perfect baby. Joe's sweet nature has persisted all his life.

This example was certainly not the only time. I say hello and talk to St. Joseph every day for his help in big and small matters, and I pray also for other people I come in contact with who have problems or who just want someone they can talk to who isn't so great and difficult to comprehend as almighty God.

Every morning, Dean and I ask St. Joseph for his prayers of intercession. I say, "St. Joseph," and Dean responds, "Pray for us." There are only two other saints whose prayers I ask for each morning: St. Vincent de Paul and the Blessed Mother. St. Joseph, St. Vincent, and Mary each prayed with us during our long series of crises. I know this because I asked them to pray for us. They only need to be asked.

One huge comfort for me during Dean's surgery was that the operation took place on March 19, the *Feast of St. Joseph*. This did not seem like a coincidence to me.

Does your family have a holy person, living or dead, to whom you feel close? Don't be afraid to ask for their prayers.

17

My Grandmother's Letters

After his stay in the hospital, Dean came home. He was terribly worried about all the time he had missed from his company, and still a little miffed that the nurses had taken his cell phone away while he was in the ICU. I had a very sick husband who was cooperating with the doctor's orders only because he wanted badly to throw himself back into the stress and fires at work.

For the first week he was home, they told us he was not to be left alone at all. He could sleep comfortably only in the lounge chair in the living room, so I camped out on the sofa each night. Family and friends came by for visits to allow me to go out to buy groceries and run errands. I stopped doing volunteer work for several weeks, learned how to balance vitamin K in Dean's diet, and drove him to follow-up appointments for rehabilitation.

Life had changed dramatically, but the prayers we had been saying about the mystery of Dean's serial illnesses had all been answered. The mystery was solved, and recuperation was ahead of us. It was at this time that I began to talk to my Grandma Agatha during prayer time. Her husband, Grandpa D'Arcy, had passed away at age thirty-four from a degenerative disease that took years to diagnose. Agatha and D'Arcy had lived with uncertainty and sickness many more years than Dean and I had, and their story had ended in death, leaving a widow with four young children in the middle of the Great Depression. "Grandma Agatha," I would say, "how did you ever cope? Please pray for us."

It was about this time that I first read my grandmother's letters.

Throughout the Depression, my grandmother Agatha was barely making ends meet, but she was determined that her children would find a way out of poverty. Money was so tight for the family that each summer Agatha turned the electricity off because she had enough funds for that luxury only during the winter. She was a prayerful woman who kept large framed pictures of the Sacred Heart and the Immaculate Heart hanging over her dining table. When thunderstorms roared through town, Agatha snatched up her holy water bottle and sprinkled the entire house, walking room to room, saying the prayer of St. Michael the Archangel. For years, she was the organist at her church, and she raised her children on hymn singing, although she had neither money nor time to give them music lessons.

In 1941, my mom, Dorothy, upon graduating from high school, was awarded a full scholarship from the Sisters of St. Joseph to attend Nazareth College in Kalamazoo, Michigan, about thirty miles from her home. She was the first in her family to attend a four-year degree program. Agatha saw this as an answer to prayer, an opportunity for her daughter to escape poverty.

That first fall term of college, freshman students were allowed to visit home only once each month, but often Dorothy couldn't afford the bus fare, and the family didn't have the dollar apiece it would cost to visit her. Talking by phone was out of the question because they didn't own one, and of course there was no family car for them to use. At one point, Agatha enclosed a dollar, borrowed from Dorothy's uncle, in a letter to her daughter so she could come home, but then she sent another letter the next day and advised her to send the money back as it was needed for some expense for her younger siblings.

So, they wrote letters (stamps cost three cents) back and forth, sometimes two or three times each week, and young, homesick Dorothy saved every one of her mother's notes.

When I read through these tiny histories, I was struck by how often Agatha mentioned prayer. Below are excerpts from the fall of 1941 and spring of 1942. They tell the story of the love of a mother whose eldest daughter is just out of physical reach but not out of the reach of written prayers.

Sept. 1941

Dear Dorothy,

How you coming? I am just sick about not being able to get over there this weekend but—money—you know. We are starting a novena* to rent the front room, so you join, please. I just have to have more money to get along. The raise was only $5 a month. I kicked to SMC [her boss; Agatha was a bookkeeper at the local hospital] but it didn't do any good . . .

*Novena: nine days of prayer for a certain intention. In this case, Agatha is asking Dorothy to pray for a boarder who will rent a room in the house now that she is away at school.

Oct. 1941

. . . I have cleaned the room and have a sign up—so now—pray!

Nov. 1941

We had a grand 40 Hours.* Fr. McCam said the rosary at the closing and Fr. McEachin was there. Seemed like old times.

*40 Hours: a devotional prayer said in the church building for forty hours straight using shifts of parishioners

Nov. 1941

. . . Shall I start worrying about your exams, too? I suppose a prayer now and then is in order.

Dec. 12, 1941 (five days after Pearl Harbor)

Well, <u>do not</u> worry about the war. Time enough when something comes along. The world has to go on and we have to keep going normally as long as we can. I suppose it is best not to have big festivities but otherwise, keep calm and pray. [Agatha's late husband, D'Arcy Wilson, served in the Canadian Army during World War I.]

March 1942

Tomorrow is your Feast Day—so Happy Day!

March 1942

May Keagle just called me (at work). Mrs. Davis died this morning at 4 o'clock. So, remember her in your prayers.

May 1942

Many thanks for my nice Mother's Day remembrance. The Spiritual Bouquet* was especially welcome as I need all those prayers and more. But you surely mortgaged your prayer time for some time to come.

*Spiritual Bouquet: a promise to say multiple prayers for the recipient. Dorothy had no money, so this was her Mother's Day gift.

May 1942

Continue your praying and a lot more fervent this week. I <u>trust</u> things will come out all right.

These precious letters give me a glimpse into my grandmother's life of poverty and prayer. She describes praying for forty hours at a clip as "grand" and about World War II as something to pray through and "keep calm" about—same as college exams and the death of a neighbor. Did she know that she was teaching her daughter about the necessity of prayer? I can only guess because she died when I was a toddler. Her letters certainly showed me the path to take when my husband became ill. Someday, I hope to have a "grand" time talking it all over with Grandma Agatha when we meet again.

While Dean was recovering his health, we still faced the stark reality of business debt. I prayed for Grandpa D'Arcy and Grandma Agatha's eternal rest, and I also asked them to pray for Dean and me as we sweated through keeping a business going during the Great Recession. They had faced many worse financial woes, and ultimately, a sadder ending to D'Arcy's illness. Who better to ask for their prayers?

Jesus said, "God is the God of the living, not of the dead"; therefore, those who have gone on ahead are living souls.

Perhaps today, you may want to write a note on your prayer list to your loved one who went on ahead. Write as if they are thirty miles away but unable to visit. Don't forget to ask them for their prayers. And when you are done, try sending a prayer text to another loved one.

18

Juan and Kana

When our daughter Ellen decided to attend Western Michigan University, on the opening day of school, the first person she met was a lovely exchange student from Japan named Kana. Ellen sat down next to her, started up a conversation, and the resulting relationship led to Ellen inviting Kana to our house for many home-cooked meals. At the end of the year, Kana invited Ellen to spend the summer in Japan with her family, and four years later, our entire family visited Kana's family over the New Year's holiday. Over the next few years, members of her family came to Michigan, and our relationships grew. We feel that Kana is our Japanese daughter.

With so many international flights in this relationship, it made for enough takeoffs, landings, and lost luggage to wear down the beads on my rosary. When one of my family is traveling, I am a diligent pray-er. Kana and her family have been the recipients of many of those Hail Marys.

Kana, like most people from Japan, was raised Buddhist and Shinto, but she also attended an all-girls Catholic grade school in her hometown. She was familiar with Christian rituals, hymns, and some of the beliefs, and it was easy to take her along with us to Christmas and Easter Mass and host her for other religious holidays.

When Kana returned to her country, graduated, and eventually took a job in Australia, we kept in contact and cheered her on. Ellen was in Japan when Kana became engaged to Juan, a young man from Mexico who was also living in Australia. The three of them arranged a rendezvous at an airport in Osaka so that Juan could be introduced to Ellen, snap photos, and send them across the world to us so we could take part in this happy occasion, too.

Today's world gives families long-distance relationships, and these relationships call for long-distance prayer. Here is Kana and Juan's story of family prayer. After a recent visit on Skype with Kana, she wrote this and sent it to me.

I met Juan in 2010 when we had both moved to Australia. I had joined a church called Hillsong, an Australian branch of the Assemblies of God (I think Hillsong is now in both LA and New York). Volunteers from our church organized an event in a café. It was based on games for practicing English. Juan and I happened to be in the same group, and it was the first time I met him. After that day, I learned that he attended the same church service, and we became friends. We got married in 2012.

Our church encourages members to join small groups that meet fortnightly during the week for fellowship and prayer. Recently, Juan and I joined a group that our friend's family leads. We have such a close relationship with them that we call them our "family" in Australia.

Juan and I had been praying for a baby since we started planning for one a few years ago. I had a few miscarriages. It had been a difficult time for us, but we kept praying together. One night, after the third miscarriage, Juan was praying, and he felt God telling him that everything was going to be fine. When I got pregnant the fourth time, I was very worried. In our small group from church, usually we pray for one another, so my friends prayed for our baby's health. The whole pregnancy was very smooth to the end. We now have Abel in our family! He is nearly one year old, and we are so happy.

We keep praying with our small group and with each other. The other night we prayed about Juan's job situation to be improved and that our friend's wife's early pregnancy will be worry-free.

I enjoy being back at work now. Abel goes to daycare next to my workplace. Actually, this lifestyle is exactly what I was praying for a few years ago; I am so blessed.

Juan and Kana bring home to me how connected the world can be: a Mexican Japanese couple living in Australia and worshipping together in a Christian megachurch. Only love can do these things. Their little Abel is one of millions of children who will grow up accepting a mix of cultures as the most natural way to live. For me, this brings great hope for our troubled world.

Today, list the different cultures, languages, denominations, religions, and ancestral countries that make up your family. Perhaps you have a family member—like our Japanese daughter, Kana—who is not actually related, but it feels that way. Put them on your list, too. Today, make your family prayer a prayer for the world.

19

Praying a Family into Being

But to those who did accept him he gave power to become children of God, to those who believe in his name, who were born not by natural generation nor by human choice nor by a man's decision but of God.
—John 1:12–13, New American Bible

When I began asking people if they had any stories to tell about family prayer, from time to time, I would hear about families who existed only because of prayer. Here are two of those stories.

You Gotta Have Faith

Judy is a lifelong, churchgoing, roll-up-her-sleeves Methodist. She volunteers at the food pantry, attends monthly women's circles, and reads Christian literature. She and her husband, John, raised two daughters and brought them up with faith and in the faith. When the youngest, Elizabeth, married and moved away, she didn't practice the practical, persevering type of religion she was raised on. She and her husband chose a more exuberant type of Christianity. Judy says: "It was fine. I admired their commitment and enthusiasm, but it wasn't the type of Christianity I was used to."

The young couple both finished their college degrees, worked and saved, and decided that it was time to start a family. But that was when their faith was tested: they were infertile. It was heartache not only for them but also for Judy and her husband. "When we were young, we had found it difficult to get pregnant, too, so I knew something about how devastated they felt," Judy remembers. "We were completely behind them when they made the decision to adopt. We thought it was a beautiful way to create a family. But . . . that didn't turn out to be easy either."

The young couple put all their savings into the applications for licenses to adopt from an orphanage in Siberia, from which many children were coming at the time. The process was long and complicated: they needed fingerprints, background checks, interviews, home visits, and endless patience. As the delays stretched out and the costs mounted, Judy and John chipped in with both prayers and finances. Then, after a year of waiting, the licenses expired, and they needed an additional five hundred dollars to renew them.

Elizabeth was speaking on the phone with her mom about this latest setback and telling her their idea for how they were going to earn the money. "I'm planning a garage sale, but it will be only books. Some of my friends have books to give me, and my colleagues at the hospital and the people at church are collecting them for us as well. We already have over a thousand. It should be perfect."

Judy listened to her daughter's bright hope for this sale and didn't say a word about how impossible it would be to sell used books for more than quarters each. But Judy didn't want to discourage her, so she said, "Well . . . that's nice, honey. When are you planning it? Maybe Dad and I can come and help you organize the books."

Elizabeth could tell from Judy's hesitation that she was humoring her. "Mom," she said, "you just gotta have faith!"

So Judy and John mustered all the faith they could and drove across two states to sort through paperback novels and picture books and then sit in lawn chairs in a driveway for two days. "It wasn't awful," she recalls. "We had fun organizing the tables, and we actually sold more books than I expected; by mid-Saturday we had netted about $125." Judy gestured at the overflowing boxes of books still sweating it out in the garage and asked Elizabeth what she wanted to do with the leftovers.

Elizabeth shook her head. "Mom, you gotta have faith. We have a lot more to sell and it's not over for an hour yet." Judy nodded and clamped her lips together.

Then a man drove up the driveway on a scooter. He had his young daughter with him, and they walked into the garage and perused the boxes' contents. After browsing, he walked up to Elizabeth and asked, "How much for all of them?"

Judy was dumbfounded.

Elizabeth said, "You want all the books?"

"Yes, I'm opening a used bookstore, and your stock will fit in well with my collection. I could give you five hundred dollars for everything. I'll bring back a truck to haul them away."

After he left, Judy was still struggling with believing what had happened, but Elizabeth was exultant. "We just needed to have faith, Mom! Isn't this amazing?" True to his word, the man returned with a truck and hauled off every volume.

While books were being scooped up in a suburban garage, George W. Bush and Vladimir Putin were not seeing eye-to-eye about world events, and, in the middle of the icy relations, Putin decided that Americans shouldn't adopt any more children out of Russia. The orphanage that had been glacially slow to process the documents suddenly rushed everything through, and, within months, Judy and her husband were among the first to welcome little redheaded Elena at the Chicago airport.

"Elena now has a younger sister, Sandra, who came from a local birth mother," Judy says. "And I can't tell you how much fun it is to be their grandma! Elizabeth was right about the faith thing."

This story comes from our friends Bess and Will. We pray for each other often, whatever the need. When Bess and I were raising teenagers, we prayed together every Wednesday while walking a labyrinth—the windy, outdoor supplications were exactly what both of us needed for that time of life. This is Bess's story about how their son came into their lives.

"Don't Go Out of Town"

Bess and Will were waiting for their baby boy to be born, but his birth mother was in every kind of distress imaginable. The lady had severe psychotic problems and gestational diabetes. She was a tiny woman who weathered one pregnancy successfully but then lost custody of the little girl. When she found out she was pregnant again (she is married), she decided to hide her condition because she was afraid that the social workers, the courts, the medical professionals, and her family would want her to have an abortion. By hiding her condition, she was far along—and had been taking her prescribed antipsychotic medications the entire time—before she received prenatal care. She did not know that the drugs would be bad and addictive for the baby. This child, the one that Bess and Will were praying for and hoping to adopt, was now under the care of the State of Michigan, the first child in the state to be removed from his parents' custody before birth.

For Bess and Will it was as if their baby were on a ship in the middle of a hurricane in the middle of the ocean.

The due date was early January, but on Thanksgiving Bess received a phone call from the adoption worker, who told her: "Don't go out of town. This baby could be here at any time." So Bess prayed, and this was her prayer: "Father, bless this child and make him strong and good."

She and Will prayed it over and over, day and night. They prayed through the Thanksgiving weekend, through the waiting weeks of

Advent, through Christmas, and through New Year's Day. "Father, bless this child and make him strong and good."

On January 6 (Epiphany), they got a call that the baby was born on the fourth and might not survive. The little boy had seizures, was in withdrawal, and there was an infection in the umbilical cord, but he was eleven pounds and strong: a prayer answered. Many people—their relatives and friends, the members of their church, people from work—began praying for him to survive. On January 10 came a call to go to the hospital and fetch him. He looked battered and had IV tubes in his head and leg, but he was strong enough to come home.

This story took place thirty-one years ago, and Mark is still strong. He lives in Beijing now, a citizen of the world. Bess and Will love him and pray the same prayer they have always prayed since that long-ago November: "Father, bless him and make him strong and good!"

God can do anything. This is true. But God doesn't do "just anything"; he's too wise for that. I think it all depends on the relationship. A father does anything that is good for his children, but sometimes children don't know what is good for them. When prayers on my list aren't answered the way I want them to be, I no longer scratch them out. Perhaps the answer will come with a man riding a scooter, or in a baby stronger than anyone could imagine.

Look at your prayer list and say a thank-you to God for the "anything" answer he is planning.

20

Car Prayers

Dean and I begin every long car trip with a prayer. We ask for a safe journey and always add, "And please keep the little animals off the road." We also have a custom of praying a Hail Mary every time we pass by the Mary statue near exit 133 on I-94. Other than that, we don't pray together in the car that much, but many families find traveling to be prime time for talking to God.

The young mother in the next story is my daughter's friend whom we have known since she was in high school. She posted this story on her Facebook page, and I replied with a request to use it in this book. Marina is not only a terrific mom, she's also a strong pray-er.

Marina is a single mom with two young daughters, Izzy (age nine) and Gigi (age five). Like many families, each morning they hustle through eating breakfast, getting dressed, and packing lunches to get into the car and drive to school and arrive at work on time. Often, after they are strapped into car seats and traveling down the road, Marina glances at their sweet faces in the rearview mirror and apologizes: "Sorry for yelling at you guys about getting out the door."

One day, she hit upon the idea that maybe car time could also be prayer time.

"We began with a Hail Mary, which they both knew, and then they worked up to saying a decade of the rosary: the Creed, the Our Father, ten Hail Marys, and the Glory Be," Marina explains. "And then, I thought—*We can say a whole rosary every day. And never miss. It will be great!* Well, that lasted about a week before we missed one, but then I told the girls we would say two the next day to catch up. Of course, they revolted, so we went back to one rosary and then decided that four decades (instead of five) fit best in the drive time. It worked for us, and the girls seemed happy with it as long as they could interrupt me for important news or to point out something in the scenery. At the end we always add, 'Mama Mary, wrap us in your mantel.' If we ever forget this line, Gigi panics and yells, 'We forgot to say Mama Mary!'"

Marina's smile is warm and hopeful despite the multiple roles of being a single mom. "The Virgin Mary is important to me, and she has always been a real person to my girls. When they were toddlers, they would carry her plastic statue around and sleep with it, something they picked up on their own." She then tells me this story:

It was almost Christmas and there was no school, so we didn't have to go out, but we hadn't seen my dad for a while. The weather was nasty sleet and very cold, but Dad told me over the phone that it was fine at his house, so I decided to chance the trip. Two to three minutes after leaving, I felt uneasy. I turned onto Thirty-Third Street, and the wheels started sliding. I couldn't do a thing, but I wasn't going very fast, so the car drifted gently into a snowbank on the side of the road and came to a halt. It seemed pretty stable, but we were perched right on the edge of a ditch. I used my cell phone to call my dad and also a friend who lived nearby. Traffic was whizzing by and each time made the car shake. Finally, a rickety van stopped behind me and a rough-looking guy smoking an e-cigarette climbed out and came up to my window. He looked at me and at the girls in the backseat and said, "Let me help. I have a tow rope in the van; maybe I can get you out of this drift."

"Oh, you don't need to do that!" I told him. "I called my Dad, and my friend is on the way with a shovel." While we were talking, several more cars whooshed past, making the car shudder.

He said, "Tell you what: I'll pull up ahead of you and see what I can do." He went back to his van, moved it around in front, got out with a rope, and knelt down to look for a place to attach it, but snow was packed too tightly under my car. The cars on the road were so close and going by so fast that I was beginning to get quite scared. He must have been feeling the same because he stood up and came to my window and said, "This is making me nervous. Let's get the kids into my car with my wife."

He was on the street side, so he opened the back door and Izzy reached out for his hand. I grabbed Gigi and got out the driver's door when I heard the man yell, "They're gonna hit!" I looked up to see a car skidding across the ice the same way I had done, so I snatched Gigi close, and all four of us sprinted up the road. Seconds later, the vehicle slammed into the side of my car where we had been standing, hit both side doors, and bounced back across the road. The girls were crying, and I threw my arms around the scruffy stranger, who still held Izzy by the hand. He hustled us into the van, and his dear wife welcomed the girls and started asking them questions about Christmas to distract them from what was going on outside. Gigi wasn't ready to be distracted. She said, "Wow! Mama Mary really did protect us in her mantel today!"

Throughout town it was a morning filled with traffic accidents, and since there were no injuries in our case, it took over an hour for the police to arrive. The man and his wife stayed the entire time—even after my dad and friend arrived—so that they could act as eyewitnesses. I had ten dollars in my purse, but they would take nothing. Waiting for the police to arrive, we all began to realize that if the man had still been in front of my car attaching the tow rope, he would have been crushed. His wife said to me, "You know, we haven't been to church in a few years, but after this, I think we're going to go."

Marina's face is soft, her voice filled with gratitude. "I badly misjudged that dear man by his appearance and still feel embarrassed by that. He had the kindest soul. Before the accident, I think I had a militant view of prayers: say them right, say them all, never skip. But now it's more like a decade of the rosary here, an Our Father there. I have to believe that God is just happy we are doing it. We can lose the meaning and the reverence with being too strict about getting it done right."

A year following the accident, Gigi earnestly asked her mom, "Are we going to get a miracle every Christmas?" Marina's story describes a young family practicing prayer not to obtain an answer or fill a request but simply to be close to God. Marina kept praying with her daughters after their rescue, but she also, wisely, backed off from perfectionism in prayer. Marina learned that praying is enough.

✎ **Do you ask God to protect your family when you travel? I often write upcoming trips on my prayer list—either mine or family members'.**

21

Rita and Gulaine

Defining the family unit is complicated. Rita is American, a nurse, and loves Christ and everyone else. Gulaine (pronounced "Goo-Lynn") is from the Democratic Republic of Congo, an aide at an assisted-living facility, and she loves Christ and everyone else, too. They are completely unrelated to each other, but they share a home, and Rita calls Gulaine her "mother" even though Rita is old enough to be hers. When I interviewed them in their kitchen, I began with Rita.

It's 1986, and Rita is inspired to travel to Kenya as a nurse on a short-term World Gospel Mission trip as part of a medical team. She falls in love with the people of East Africa and desires to make it her life's calling to work there, but this is not to be. At home in Michigan, her already disabled mother is diagnosed with Alzheimer's disease, and her father needs her help. Rita returns to the United States, moves in with her parents, and stays from 1991 to 1996. After her mother's passing, Rita learns of another medical mission trip through the World Gospel Mission to Tenwek Hospital, northwest of Nairobi. Her Christian Reformed Church agrees to sponsor her for part of the cost, but it isn't enough. This is when Rita's family steps up.

"My church was praying, I was praying, but everything looked closed to me because I didn't have nearly enough money to participate. I don't think of my family as being all that prayerful," says Rita. "But when this opportunity came up, they knew it was my dream, so they pooled money in honor of my mother to defray my costs, and called it the Ruth Albertson Memorial Fund. It was what I needed to go back to Africa." All these years later, she wipes away tears, remembering her extended family's support. "I was able to stay there from January 1997 to July 1999. I will always be grateful."

After fulfilling her dream, Rita returned to Michigan and settled down, bought a home, and went back to an ordinary life—except she had extra bedrooms. She smiles and says: "Ever since living there, I am always attracted to people from Africa. Right now, I have a young woman from Kenya living with me. She has graduated from nursing school and is studying to take her state boards. Next, Gulaine came as a refugee from Congo in 2016, but she was living temporarily with another family. We happened to be in church on the same day, sitting near each other. During the handshake of peace, I met her and invited her to come to my birthday party that afternoon. I learned that she needed a more permanent home, and from there everything came together."

Gulaine describes the circumstances this way: "I was in a refugee camp, and when the opportunity came for me to go to the United States, I prayed to God, 'Please, Lord, I want a family that knows you—one that prays.' I couldn't tell the government caseworker this because prayer is not how they place people; they will give you to who they will." She recalls her life of prayer in war-torn Congo. "I am Catholic, and we pray a prayer called the Angelus at noon and at midnight. I also love to pray the Divine Mercy Chaplet at 3 p.m. and at 3 a.m. In Congo, every day I would wake up in the middle of the night and pray for my family and everyone else: my friends, those who don't know God, the ones who need peace—the entire world. I told all my troubles to my 'Daddy' and he comforted me." She pulls up her skirt a little and shows me her knees, which have round calluses on them about the size of a half dollar. "I pray on my knees to my Daddy. My life is prayer. I love God because he makes a way when I am in a difficult problem and I believe he can help me. When I was coming here, I prayed, 'Give me a job and a praying family.' I got the job at the assisted-living home, and Rita gave me a praying home, but there was a big problem because I didn't have transportation to work. My shift began at 6 a.m., but the buses didn't begin running early enough to get me there on time. I called the taxi companies, but it was fifteen dollars for the trip and my salary was so little. Someone told me about Uber, but the drivers only begin work at 7 a.m. What to do? I prayed, 'God, you didn't bring me here to suffer. You brought me here so people will know you are the Lord. You gave me the job, so you can give me the solution to this transportation problem.'"

"I told my supervisor the problem, and she asked, 'Are you leaving, Gulaine?' I said, 'No. I am praying.'"

"Later that week, my supervisor came to me and said, 'A worker canceled for the night shift tonight. Can you take her place? I will give you a ride if you can help me out.' I thought, *at night*? I won't sleep! Maybe I will lose my time for prayer! But my supervisor said, 'I need your help; please come.' So, I agreed to help that night."

Gulaine smiles and raises her hands in joy. "The shift ran from 10 p.m. to 6 a.m., and I could catch the metro bus at both of those times. Also, I could take my breaks at midnight and at 3 a.m. There is a laundry room that is quiet and empty during the night, so I could kneel and pray. My supervisor came to me more and more and asked me to help on the night shift, and I began to feel happier, just a little. But I kept quiet. Then God changed the shift for me. I asked the supervisor if I could work always at night, and she was so happy!"

Gulaine looks very serious when she says the next thing. "God is the God of fifty-nine minutes and fifty-nine seconds."

I ask, "Excuse me? He is what?"

"He is the God of all situations. He will come at the last second, and at the end of time. God has more plans for me. To go to sleep and to wake up is a miracle. Look at so many people in hospitals—they sleep and don't wake up. Every day I wake up, I say, 'Thank you, Lord!' In Matthew 6, it says to go to your room, shut the door, and pray. What does that mean? It means leave everything behind when you pray. It means pray in secret and in silence, and he will answer you in secret and in silence. For this reason, I pray at night; it's a quiet time to be with my father."

"In laundry rooms," I repeat.

She beams. "Yes."

"Do you always pray alone?"

"No, not at all. I pray with people all over the world. My friends in Africa, some of them in Europe, here in this country, they ask me to call them at midnight or at three in the morning, and we pray together, six to ten of us each night. I don't call them all, just a couple each time, but I know that they are praying with me. Rita picks me up after my shift on the mornings when she doesn't work. We sit in the car together and pray."

Rita smiles and explains: "She doesn't complain. We don't talk about difficulties—we pray about them. She is a wise woman because she uses her energy to pray. Every day, she teaches me something—she is my mother." Rita reaches for her Bible and shows me the papers tucked inside. "I make papers in the shape of eggs and write my prayers on them, then I put them in the Bible until they are 'hatched.' When the prayers are answered, Gulaine says, 'You don't know if you are going to wake up tomorrow, so don't forget to be grateful for the answered prayers—keep them in your Bible as a reminder.'"

Gulaine's smile is warm and calm. "I like to pray with others because of their experiences of prayer. They remind me of people in the Bible. Opening the word of the Lord makes me stronger. Opening the Bible is like eating pizza—it's so good, so sweet! Rita is my daughter, so every day I give her the verse from the Bible that is on my heart. To share the word of the Lord makes us stronger. God said, 'If two or three pray in my name, I am present.' Every day God knows what he will do for me. If I make plans, I say also, 'If God wishes.' Each day comes with its own grace from God."

Rita and Gulaine write their prayers on egg-shaped papers and incubate them between the pages of the Bible until they are hatched. Isn't that the best prayer list ever?

22

"She Was Wearing a Blue Dress!"

Deena started out as my sister's friend before she became mine. She told me this story three years ago, long before I began writing this book. I hadn't seen her in a while, and I wasn't sure if I had her contact information, so I said to God during morning prayer time: "Do you want Deena's story in this book? If you do, help me figure out how to find her phone number." Then I drove to Mass, and Deena walked in and sat down across the chapel from me.

Well, that was clear!

Christmas 2014 was a very emotional time for our family. Our eighty-seven-year-old father had been diagnosed with melanoma just before Thanksgiving and was given two to three months to live. Mom and Dad lived one hundred miles north of their five children, but we all rallied around them and made sure Dad could spend his last days in his own home. Hospice was wonderful, and the hospice workers reassured us whenever we phoned with questions about Dad's care. On December 16, my niece and I were talking with Dad, and he was trying to console us. He did tell us that he would be going home whenever God was ready for him. Tearfully, I asked if he could possibly stay with us until Christmas because that was when one of my sons in

Texas and two nephews in Colorado were coming home. Dad gently reminded us that he would be going when God wanted him home.

Our father was a beautiful example of what a Catholic father should be. When he learned he was terminal, he asked for his parish priest, so he could make his last confession. Mom and I are eucharistic ministers, and he received communion as often as possible. Dad was not suffering with a lot of pain, and so the decision had been made to not take pain medication.

On Christmas Eve, at our traditional Christmas celebration, Dad asked to speak to us individually and gave each of us a personal message. My parents always gave the grandchildren gifts at Christmas, and for this one Dad had asked me to find rosaries for each of them.

My mother had always said the rosary daily, but Dad joined her only occasionally. After the diagnosis, he would say it with her every evening. No matter what was happening or who was visiting, he would gather everyone in the house together, and they would all pray.

One night, at the end of the rosary, Dad had a vision of our Blessed Mother.

My brother said that Dad was peacefully praying the glorious mysteries with them, lying in his bed, which was raised up a bit. All of a sudden, he sat bolt upright and started exclaiming about the vision. He was very excited, and tears were streaming from his eyes. My brother was not sure how to respond, perhaps being skeptical that it was a vision. He could see that Dad was overwhelmed by the experience.

Dad called those of us who were not with him and told us about the vision. He told me that Mary was the most beautiful woman he had ever seen and that she was wearing blue. I cried when he said that, partially because of the emotion in his voice, but mostly because *my dad is colorblind*. He has always been colorblind, and yet he could see the shade of her dress.

Dad passed away peacefully on January 3, 2015, with my mom, all five of his kids, and three of his grandkids around him.

 Take blue, red, green, or any color markers and doodle with joy all around your prayer list while you pray today.

23

A Pink Box

My friend has dealt with mental illness for more than thirty years. She is under the treatment of medical professionals and counselors and values their caring help. She lives alone in an apartment that meets her needs, but she would like to move. The apartment is safe, but her illness often makes her feel afraid. "Voices" in her head tell her mean things, and it is a struggle every day to push those voices away. I asked her if she has any stories to tell me about family prayer, and this is what she said:

"I have a pink prayer box. It's not fancy, just a cloth box with no lid. When someone asks me to pray for them, like my sisters or friends, I write it on a notepad because, if I don't, I will forget. My illness has caused some cognitive problems, so it makes it hard for me to remember things. I put the little notes in my box, and every day I pull them out and pray. I also have my Bible in the box, a daily devotional book, and about twenty holy cards with prayers on them that I say every day."

"I have dark days, so sometimes it comforts me to say the Memorare to the Blessed Virgin Mary and the Prayer to St. Michael the Archangel. I always read the ninety-first Psalm because it protects me. If I'm depressed, I try to fall asleep saying my prayers."

My friend gets quiet and seems pensive. "The 'voices' sometimes tell me that I am going to hell. If I never see my parents again, I would feel sad. Last week I was feeling this way, and I prayed, 'God, please don't send me to hell!' I pulled out my devotional, and the reading told me that God was just beginning to have a relationship with me. When I read that, the thought came to me, *You're going to heaven!* It was so different from the other voices. I felt very comforted by this. I'll take that voice over the mean ones any day!"

When the biggest crises were over, after Dean's surgery, after the long recovery, after the bills were paid—our daughter Ellen said to me, "Ma, I really appreciate that you didn't fall apart. We could only do what we did to help because you were holding it together."

I'm pretty sure I wasn't the one holding myself together.

It was the prayer that was surrounding me and coming from our family and friends that kept me functioning. Why do I believe this? Because nine months later, when the business was sold and Dean went to work for the new owners, and Martha had a new job, and I wasn't asking people for prayers any longer, it was then that I began having issues with anxiety. My sleep was terrible; I was having back spasms; more often than not, my teeth were clenched; and anger bubbled up in situations that had never provoked me before. I was dealing with symptoms I thought I had outrun.

I called my friend with the pink prayer box who faces anxiety nearly every day, and she agreed to meet me for lunch. The advice she gave me came from a group counseling session she attends. Here it is: "Excuse instead of accuse for your own mental health."

Ah.

She may as well have said, "Forgive us our trespasses as we forgive those who trespass against us" or any number of similar prayers that

I recite every day. She helped me see that prayer could be a path to recovering my footing. Prayer had held me together in the ICU, and prayer might help lead me out of my present state of anxiety, too.

But I had never stopped praying, so what was I missing? The prayer list helped me pray for my loved ones—was there a way it could help me pray for myself?

An old African American spiritual says, "Not my brother, not my sister, but it's me, O Lord, standing in the need of prayer. Not my mother, not my father, but it's me, O Lord, standing in the need of prayer. It's me, it's me, O Lord, standing in the need of prayer. It's me, it's me, O Lord, standing in the need of prayer."

Today, put yourself on your prayer list.

24

Statues and Icons in Family Prayer

We have some pieces of religious art in our home. One time, a guest walked in, glanced around, and said, "I get the impression that someone who lives here is Catholic."

Dean thought this was pretty funny. "Yes," he said, "and she's one hundred percent with the program."

We have a lovely print of the Madonna in the living room, a crucifix in the bedroom, an icon of St. Francis hangs in the kitchen, and St. Anthony is in the laundry room (for all those missing socks). During Christmastime, things pick up speed.

When Dean was in the hospital, I tucked some holy cards in my purse to pray with during the long hours of waiting. They helped me wait. I'll take that.

This story is from my friend Peggy's daughter, Kathleen, who holds a doctorate in geography and travels extensively. She is a woman who prays for her family and for the whole wide world that she loves. I first met her black Madonna statue when Our Lady was residing in the middle of Peggy's dining table for several weeks.

The Black Madonna Traveling in the Family

I think my mother remembers this story better than I do. I suppose that is the gist of any story about family: the story and the storytelling are communal.

I was in Zimbabwe and wanted to bring home this statue of the Virgin Mary holding the baby Jesus. She was hand-carved at Drufontane mission, a tiny outpost in the dry, sandy eastern part of Zimbabwe. The mission was dedicated to teaching orphaned deaf boys wood carving. The youngest children carved the smallest statues; as the boys grew in skill and strength, they carved larger and larger ones. The most stunning examples were life-sized or larger: a crucified Christ, Joseph, angels, and an absolute wealth of black Madonnas in every size. Some had already been promised to churches around the world and were sitting in the sand, waiting for shipment. I chose my statue based on the limitations of getting her back home. Twenty-four inches was the largest size that I could safely wrap in dirty laundry and pack into my luggage, my dad's Vietnam-era army duffle.

After I got home I learned—as I am sure countless others have learned before me—that, for Mary, being submissive to God never meant being submissive to anyone's preconceptions or staying quietly at home. It was clear, somehow, that "she" (the statue was definitely a "she" and no longer an "it" at this point) wanted to keep traveling. And so she went to live with my mother for a while, and with my younger sister after that, traveling from place to place in the backseat of our car, held safe by a seatbelt.

My mom remembers this so clearly—twenty years ago now—perhaps because it was within a year of my moving out of the house. My parents became empty nesters. Maybe we were all concerned that our stories would stop being communal. But family stories never stop being communal. We share our experiences, our hopes, our prayers, and our aids to prayer, and we share a mysterious connection to a deaf Shona boy named HERBERT, whose name is carved in bold block letters on the base of our black Madonna.

The three long years of stress were beginning to resolve, and some of the pressure had lifted, but the lingering anxiety I was feeling needed to be faced. I realized this when, after another too-tense, angry, back-spasm week, I was talking with Martha on the phone. She listened patiently to the stress in my voice and said, "Mom, even the pope quit."

Oh.

That was true. Pope Benedict had resigned, breaking with centuries of tradition.

That weekend I prayed about it, and then I made the decision to change my life.

I stepped back from too much work and volunteering to take better care of myself and my family. I also knew that I needed to spend more time with God. For the first time in my life, I heaped gobs of time into silence, meditation, and prayer. And I began to exercise regularly to deal with the back problem. The anxiety and sleeplessness made me realize that I did not have life all figured out, and the odd feeling I got from my prayer time was that God was fine with that.

The prayer list became a symbol of this not-knowing.

For, what are prayers of petition except all the questions we are asking God? "Why did Dean get sick?" "God, which job should Martha apply for?" "When will this back pain end?" "When should I start volunteering again?" The prayer list was a way to ask the questions, but God's reply consistently seemed to be, "You don't need to know that, Jane."

At first, this low-speed life didn't feel like enough. I missed helping people through volunteer work. Was I being lazy? Shouldn't I get more done? My prayer time was deliciously restful: shouldn't it be more fervent?

In fact, I had an uneasy feeling about taking so much time for prayer.

Prayer, rest, and peaceful relationships couldn't possibly be what God wants. Or could it? I began to wonder if the point of prayer might be less about asking God to change circumstances or solve problems and more about changing me. Was it possible that God wanted me to sit still so he could move in my life? That he wanted me to be quiet so he could be heard?

One day, Tania, whom I had recently met, messaged me on my phone. She had read my book and wondered if I would care to go out for coffee. I couldn't remember the last time I had done that, but sure—why not? Through quiet, peaceful conversations about prayer and God, effortlessly, she and I became friends. Then Amy called, another person I was getting to know, and after that, I gradually became a regular at local breakfast places where family members, new acquaintances, and long-neglected friends began to generously share time with me. The oddest thing happened: my prayer list became not merely two columns of names on a pad of paper, but it also transformed into warm, kind faces sitting across a table sipping tea and coffee.

My life changed from high-charged "doing" for others into peaceful "being" with others.

One unexpected blessing of this change was that many stories in this book came from these simple conversations with friends and family. Not only were my loved ones on a physical prayer list, but I also had more time to spend with them and listen to their concerns.

I am certain that prayer changes things. At least, it changed me.

I hope you enjoy Tania's story about how her family prays with religious medals and icons—she is special to me.

A Prayer Book Full of Smudges

Grandma was of Armenian ancestry. She and Grandpa immigrated to the United States from Lebanon when she was in her sixties, following her son (my father) who had come over and established himself here a few years earlier.

Grandma's faith was extremely important to her because of what was going on with all the Armenian people at the time. My parents were not as religious as my grandmother. They didn't have me baptized as an infant because they wanted me to be fully aware of what I was getting into and to choose for myself.

When I was growing up, Grandma and Grandpa lived in an apartment house for seniors. I can picture clearly all her religious articles, especially the ones in her bedroom. Hanging above her bed was a picture of Jesus, Mary, and Joseph, and draped over that was the brown scapular. Also, nearby was an oval picture of the Sacred Heart with writing around it in Latin. And, of course, she always had palms from the Palm Sunday Mass.

Grandma was not what I would call a dogmatic Catholic. When we talked about religion, she never talked about anything political. All she ever talked about was praying. When she was old and couldn't get to church, she made sure to take time for prayer on Sundays.

When I began my spiritual searching and decided to get baptized at age twenty-three, I asked Grandma if she would be my sponsor. She agreed that she would, but she was curious about the instruction I was getting. "So, did you learn your prayers?" she asked.

"Huh?" I was confused. I thought that maybe she was referring to the Our Father, Hail Mary, and Glory Be—the kind of things they teach children. I was learning about the sacraments, liturgy, church history, and social justice. When I didn't rattle off the prayers, Grandma made one of her faces, but she wasn't one to rock the boat, so she let it pass. It was a wonderful day when she sponsored me to join the Church. My parents attended the ceremony, and they were fine with it, but Grandma was probably the most pleased by my decision.

At one point, I needed some neck surgery. Grandma brought over a medal from Lourdes in France. She put it on my neck and prayed over me. When she was finished, I asked, "Oh, can I have that?"

"No," she said. "I still need it."

Grandma always made sure that all of us in the family had a picture of Jesus in the glove compartment of our cars for safety. She gave one to my parents, and they put it in their car without objecting. When I bought my first car, she gave me one and of course I did the same.

One day, I had a car accident. Grandma came to see me and asked, "Did you have Jesus' picture in the glove compartment? How can something like this happen to you?!"

"Yes," I told her. "I had the picture." She couldn't understand how I could have been hurt with the picture of Jesus in the car, but I was thinking, *Well, I don't know, maybe it could have been worse?*

My parents have come to a place in their lives where, although they don't attend church regularly, they do visit a shrine called Little Rose, which is under the ecclesiastical protection of the Autonomous Ukrainian Orthodox Church in America. They light candles for prayer, and my mom picks up holy water for me to put in my wall fonts.

When Grandma passed away, she had given directions to put her rosary and daily prayer book in the casket with her. But she left me her prayer book about the saints. I was so happy to have it. When

I opened it up for the first time, I noticed that all the pictures had smudges on them. I looked closer to figure out what had caused it.

There were lipstick marks on each picture.

Do you have a piece of religious art in your home or garden? How does it help your family pray?

25

Praying with Dead Family Members

Are there risks in talking to dead family members? Sure. If I conjure them up with the purpose of hearing from them or getting something from them in return, then I am pitting myself against God. We all belong to God, and if he has decided to separate us for a time through death, and if we try to sneak around the arrangement, we will be up against God's will. This is not the type of prayer I am talking about in this chapter. I am not advocating séances.

The tradition of praying for dead people and of asking for their prayers is common in the Catholic faith. Where does this come from? Jesus met Moses and Elijah on the mountain, an incident recorded in Matthew 17:2, Mark 9:2–8, Luke 9:28–36, and 2 Peter 1:16–18. The three had a conversation. Nowhere is it written that Jesus asked them to come back from the dead and talk with him. They apparently came while he was praying silently.

Jesus also told his friends to "follow me." So, it seems clear that it is fine to talk to people who have gone on ahead of us. We can even have a conversation with them if they initiate it. Even though it isn't recommended that we ask them to do things for us—we should ask only God—it's long been a tradition to ask them to pray for us. They are, after all, our loved ones who prayed for us while in the flesh. And since prayer is talking with God, our loved ones are as capable of praying for us after death as they were before. Why would we not pray for them in return? Death is not a reason to stop praying for people. In the Catholic tradition, the Hail Mary is a prayer that specifically asks Jesus' mother to "pray for us now and at the hour of our death."

Mary Karen Kabisch McClellan is a cyberfriend of mine who connected with me on social media because of the other books I have written. Our relationship dwells on the little screens of our phones and desktops, and we delight one another with humorous posts and shared concern for the suffering members of society. I wouldn't recognize her if we sat down together on a church pew.

I saw this post on her Facebook page when I was in the middle of writing this book, and I thought, That is a good story about praying with the dead, but I know her only casually and maybe it is weird to ask her to share it in a book, and it would be awkward to contact her, and praying with the dead is über-Catholic, and, and, *and . . . So I quickly talked myself out of contacting her. I touched the "like" button and moved on.* The very next day, *Mary sent a message to my account, informing me that she had given my first book to a friend. This was the only time she had ever contacted me directly.*

"Okay, God," I said. "I'll play along."

I hit the reply button and asked her if I could use her story.

I'm pretty certain this story is supposed to be here. It is in Mary's own words, just like her cyber post.

"Get Down on Your Knees"

My mother was Italian and very verbose. People either found her amazing due to her strength or were really put off by her. When she passed, I was heartbroken. There was a huge snowstorm that week, and we moved all her belongings into a room in our basement. I had a hard time going through her things. I would cry.

Eventually, I dug into them and found a great deal of money that her friends gave toward Masses to be said for her. I took the few hundred dollars to my parish and scheduled the Masses. However, my congregation is very large, with many requests made for memorial Masses, so my mother's memorials were put on the calendar long before they would occur.

At that time in my life, I had gotten rather lazy with my prayers. I would say them lying down in bed, often falling asleep before finishing my rosary. One night, as I was saying my "lazy" prayers I heard a voice say, "Get down on your knees." I was startled and popped down to my knees. Needless to say, my prayer was much better. At the end, I heard the same voice say, "Go to Mass tomorrow." I looked up the time for morning Mass and went the next day. As the Mass began, the priest announced that it was being said for Mary Lou Kabisch.

I froze. *What?!*

I hadn't noticed that it was July 12 and my mother's birthday. Many months prior, in the middle of winter, I had requested the Mass be said for her but had since then totally forgotten about it.

To this day, I say my prayers on my knees.

The next story is from my fellow parishioner Patricia at St. Joseph Church in Kalamazoo, Michigan. She is the one who helps collect hats and mittens for the kids who attend the public school across the street from the church. She takes communion to the homebound and people in nursing homes. When the parish needs a reception, she knows all the cooks and makes sure the tables are full of casseroles. She does a lot of other loving things, but she is so quiet about it that I become aware of her good works only when I stumble upon her doing them. Pat has had more than her share of family troubles to pray about, but that doesn't keep her from praying for others. Her family prayer story upgraded my understanding of praying with our dead loved ones.

"Do You Want to Dance?"

When Pat came into her enormous Italian family, it had resided only two generations in this country. She has beautiful memories of praying with her mother, a woman who was forced into an arranged marriage at age fifteen and divorced from two husbands. When she was forty-three and her children were ages eighteen and twenty-four, she adopted Pat as a one-day-old infant.

"My mom, Mary, and I prayed together every evening. We would sit down in the living room, and our dog Butch would come and lie next to us. Then, the cat Smokey would climb onto the dog's back, and the parakeet Petey would land on the cat. They would stay stacked up like that the whole time we prayed! Mom and I prayed our night prayers together until I got married and moved out of the house. We prayed mostly for family members who were ill; I remember especially praying for my grandma after her stroke. While Grandma was in the hospital, the entire clan showed up regularly: twenty kids and ten adults, all praying aloud in the room. In my family, we are not shy about praying together."

When Mom was ninety-one years old, she lived in an assisted-living facility near me in Michigan. My older sister and brother had moved to different states, but I could visit Mom every day. One Friday when my sister was visiting, we took Mom to her doctor because she had a bad cough. The doctor diagnosed pneumonia and ordered an antibiotic, but he didn't suggest taking her to the hospital. As we were leaving, he said to me, "Pat, when you leave here, in the next couple of days, get in touch with hospice so they can come and evaluate her."

I said, "Okay . . . ?" and waited for more explanation, but that was all he said. I decided he was being cautious because Mom was so elderly. On the way home, we were driving by a relative's house and Mom was feeling a little tired but otherwise fine, so we stopped in for a visit and afterward took her back to her place.

My sister was planning to fly home to Houston the next day, but I felt uneasy, so I told her that maybe she should think about staying another day or two. But she had a lot of things scheduled at home, Mom seemed fine, and so she left. On Sunday, the assisted-living facility called me and said my mother wasn't feeling well. I went over there and walked into her room. "What's going on, Mom?" I asked.

She said, "I don't know, but I saw my mom last night."

Grandma passed away in 1963. My mom kept a nice photo of her on the buffet nearby. Maybe she was confused about the picture? I asked, "Where did you see her? Over there?" and I pointed to the photo.

"No, I saw *her*—not the picture. She was up in the corner of the room, where the wall meets the ceiling. She was beckoning to me with her hands."

I looked at the top of the wall and, of course, nothing was there. "Did she talk?" I asked.

"No. She didn't say anything."

"Is Grandma here now?"

"No. As soon as you came in, she was gone."

I decided that maybe I would stay around. We turned on the TV and watched for a while. During a commercial, Mom said, "Did you go to church today?"

"Of course. You know I go every week."

"Did you pray for me?"

"Yes, I did. I prayed for everybody in the family like we always do." Mom seemed good despite this odd conversation. She wasn't struggling to breathe, she was enjoying the TV show, and otherwise seemed normal. Yet I didn't want to leave her. I told her I would go home and get an overnight bag and come back, but she insisted that I didn't need to and that she was fine.

The next morning, I called the front desk of the facility from my job. They said that the hospice people had brought a hospital bed, but Mom hadn't been disturbed by it. Late in the morning, they called me to say that Mom wasn't herself, but there were no specific problems. I left work and drove over there.

When I walked into the room, she was sitting in her chair, and she knew me as usual and asked about my husband and the dog. I felt relieved that she was on top of things, but I stayed around to chat anyway. At one point, she smiled at me and asked, "Do you want to dance?"

I stared at her. "Do I . . . *what?*" In her youth, my mom had been fond of dancing, but that was a long time ago.

"How about the jitterbug?" she asked.

"Do you really want to dance, Mom?"

"Yes," she said, "but not in the hallway—just here in the room."

I suggested a waltz instead of the jitterbug, and that was fine with her. I put on some music, she stood up, and we danced all around her room; slow and easy because she was weak, but we danced.

When the music ended, she was tired and wanted to get into the hospice bed. I called my husband and told him I wasn't coming home and to bring me an overnight bag. By 4 p.m. Mom was resting peacefully, but she kept looking up at the corner of the room. Then she started having a conversation without me.

"Hi, Mom," she said, then paused. "Well, no, I don't know about that."

I asked her, "Who are you talking to?"

"Grandma! You can't see Grandma? She's right there." And she gestured up to the ceiling.

The hospice worker walked in and told me that my mother was not doing well. I said, "What do you mean 'not doing well'? She was dancing this afternoon." The worker didn't argue with me. I spent the night. I slept in Mom's bed with her and held her in my arms.

The next morning, the hospice people told us, "Your mother is actively in the dying stage. It's best to call the relatives to come." I called my brother and sister, and they couldn't believe it—she had been so well the week before.

Wednesday, we prayed and prayed, and I was crying at times. Mom asked me, "Why are you so sad?"

"I don't know," I lied.

She said, "I know I'm dying. Don't you see Grandma?"

I shook my head.

"She's here to show me the way. I think she's taking me to heaven."

"No, Mom," I said.

"What? You think maybe I'm going to hell instead?!" And she smiled.

People came and went all day— we have a big family—maybe thirty or more visitors.

Late that night, she asked me, "Are you going to be all right?" This was the moment when I finally knew that she was leaving.

I said to her, "I'm not going to be all right for now . . . but I'll be okay."

She said "okay" and never spoke again. At seven in the morning, she died peacefully in my arms—no pain, a little restless at times, but not struggling. I'm certain Grandma came to get her.

Add a few dead family members to your prayer list today.

26

"A Breakthrough from Soul to Soul"

Fr. Mike has been our parish priest for most of my adult life. He is the type of priest who is excellent in the confessional as well as the pulpit, and everyone wants him to officiate at their funeral. I can tell him the worst about myself, and yet I know he will do his best to pray me into heaven. Forgiveness and love pour out of this man.

Slowly, after I'd taken nearly a year off from volunteering, Fr. Mike and a couple of St. Vincent de Paul friends invited me back into the "doing" side of prayer. Dean was healthy, and I had regained a reliable calm, so we both returned to doing volunteer work in our community. But this time, we limited the time spent on meetings, focused on face-to-face contact with those in need, and placed parentheses of prayer at both ends of everything we did. Fr. Mike's counsel kept us reaching for God's guidance through prayer before we put one foot in front of another.

I didn't think of asking him for a family prayer story because he is the person who leads me in corporate, church prayer. He also advises me on private prayer and meditation, whereas family prayer is something I do outside of church. But I was near the end of gathering these stories when a fellow parishioner said, "You should ask Fr. Mike about praying with his brother Vern. He told the story in Vern's eulogy, and it was very touching." That was enough recommendation for me.

For background, I asked Fr. Mike to describe his experience of family prayer when he was growing up. The first half of this chapter is Fr. Mike's remembrances. The second half is an edited version of his homily notes for Vern's funeral.

Successful in Family Love

Our parents, Flora and Tom, "Mom" and "Pop," were family pray-ers for as long as I can remember. We prayed the rosary together some Octobers or Mays, the months in which Mary is especially acknowledged. In the 1950s, they went weekly to devotional services focused on Mary as Our Mother of Perpetual Help, and sometimes I went along. As a family we never missed Sunday Mass and rarely missed the prayer before meals. Sometime in the 1960s, our parents became daily pray-ers of the rosary. But we never had a spontaneous prayer together unless—after I had been in the seminary for a half dozen years—I was entrusted with leading the grace before meals. My father's sister, Aunt Lucille, was a member of the Church of the Nazarene. She was the family member who shared faith and prayer with me as I grew into adulthood—and often that was by letter back and forth between Michigan and Florida.

It was very rare for my dad to say, "I love you" to any of his kids. On his deathbed, he said that to me, and I didn't know how to respond.

Vern had come to a place in his life, several years ago, when he, like families on TV, would conclude a phone conversation with, "Love you." "Love you, too." I'm not sure about his relationships with other family members but with me, Vern was, I don't know, sort of unwilling, unable to reveal himself. Mostly we talked about the little dogs in the house, or the yard that needed mowing, or something. I suppose I didn't say too much about myself, either.

Until that day at the memory-care facility, we had never prayed together, just the two of us.

Vern Paul Hazard +3/8/1929 Funeral 7/1/2017
Scriptures
Lamentations 3:17–26 *I will keep this in mind as my reason to have hope.*
Psalm 103 *The Lord is kind and merciful.*
1 John 4:7–16 *If we love one another, God remains in us.*
Mark 12:28–31 *There is no other commandment greater than these.*

†   †   †

He was his father's son—I mean, Vern was Tom Hazard's son. And he was *his* father's son. Six of us (Vern, Joe, Anne, Cathy, Alice, and I) descended from the same father and mother. Vern broke in Mom and Pop for the rest of us—well, he and our brother, Joe. These two, Vern Paul and Joseph Thomas, born fourteen months apart, were a dynamic duo. I suspect they communicated with one another, even as toddlers, in ways that empowered them to terrorize their parents. Whatever the whole truth of it may be, these two did a good job of teaching Tom and Flora that kids are not as fragile as maybe they thought. By the time I came along, fifteen years later, life was pretty relaxed, relatively speaking.

Does the word *pranking* mean anything to you? Well, it was a lifestyle choice for my oldest brother. I believe he learned this from our dad, Tom Hazard; and that he learned it from *his* father. Vern's childhood was spent in the company of both of these pranksters for most of his first ten or more years—a very impressionable time for a lad. Vern was a really gifted guy: clever, insightful, intelligent, hardworking. With little schooling beyond high school, he learned the arcane workings of calculus. He was interested in new things—technology and gadgets and ideas. . . . The son of his father, he had a sort of deficit in expressing affection—they were born in another millennium.

I'd like to share with you one of two really personal conversations I had with my brother. I went to the assisted-living memory-care place where he was living—about fourteen months ago. When I found him, we went to his room; a pretty spacious place, as such rooms go, adorned with portraits of family members, mostly. He was comfortable there, he in his wheelchair and I in another chair in front of him. During the next forty-five minutes, Vern directed the conversation. His condition was such that he was able to use English sentence structure and some elements of content to give me an idea where his mind was trying to go. For those forty-five minutes, he often went to religious topics, in deference to the clergyman in the room. I was not entirely sure that he was crystal-clear about my identity—he asked me, for instance, whether I had seen my mother today (our mother died thirty years ago).

When it was getting to be supper time and the conversation was waning, I volunteered, "Would it be okay if I offered a prayer for us?"

His reply: "I was thinking that would be a good idea."

I crossed the few steps between us and bent over him, with my arms around his shoulders and my mouth close to his ear. When I finished the prayer, which I think might have been on themes of family love and God's care, I stood and could see that he was crying softly. He looked up—not at me, really—and said, "I always hoped you would be successful."

If I can take advantage now of being the designated preacher for today, let me say that Vern's words carry a very God-like sentiment. God's hope, God's dream for us, is that we may be "successful" in the most human venture: family love. God has always been working toward that destiny we call Heaven. God's dream and the object of God's work is that we be enveloped in the Spirit of Love that binds the Father Almighty and the Eternal Son in Communion. This communion we begin to recognize in the very best moments of our love for one another: moments when we can forget about ourselves in gratitude, or in awe, or in mercy.

Moments when there's a breakthrough from soul to soul, heart to heart: generosity, tenderness, guard down, no foolin', no pranking for now.

And each of us, as we are able to receive the grace of that transformation, each of us is being drawn into a love that is more trusting and more obedient to the divine image in which we were created and which sin mucks up. When our souls are deprived of peace and we have forgotten what happiness is, we too must keep this in mind as our reason to have hope: *The favors of the Lord are not exhausted; God's mercies are never spent.* Every morning they are renewed; so great is God's faithfulness.

The law of love is written not principally on tablets of stone but in human hearts. Loving God with all our heart and soul and strength really means trusting the love of God that awakens love in us; trusting enough to follow the way of love in our relationships with one another.

The success God dreams for us sees small but wonderful moments of fulfillment when we are able—even for forty-five minutes, even for a single minute—to focus our attention with generosity and care and tenderness on one another. These are moments of grace that help us experience even now a taste of the heaven to which we are called, by the generosity and tender love of God for us in Jesus.

I asked Fr. Mike what Vern was looking at when he said, "I always hoped you would be successful." Fr. Mike answered: "I think he was just looking up and out, not at me. I do think he was talking to me; but he was revealing something he had never told anyone before, and may have been—strange as this may sound—afraid of being laughed at or something. I believe that prayer changes things, but so do changes in your health, family circumstances, and plenty of other influences."

In your prayer list today, write the names of loved ones with whom you have rarely shared a personal prayer. As Fr. Mike knows, sometimes it's just too personal to pray with our own family members. Begin today by praying *for* them.

27

Door to Door

According to Jesus' parable, God is the sower of the seed and we are the field where he plants. It is our job to cultivate the ground, and one way we can do that is through prayer. God can drop bags and bags of good seed, but if we fail to water it or feed it with good soil, it simply won't take root. Our families and the people we meet each day are a field to cultivate, too. We aren't expected to cultivate the entire world by ourselves, either. Sure, we should pray for the world, but the field we are most responsible for is the little one surrounding us.

When looking for stories about family prayer, I purposely did not search the entire world. I went about it by asking my family and friends for their stories. I prayed about it and trusted God to give me the stories.

Praying seemed like a no-brainer way to go about writing a book about prayer.

My acquaintances frequently ask me about what I am currently writing. When this book was in the works, I would answer, "I'm writing a book about family prayer. Do you have a story for me?"

Isn't it fascinating that from a little corner of Michigan, in an average size city, stories came to me from Florida, Indiana, Illinois, Wisconsin, Kenya, the Democratic Republic of Congo, France, Germany, Algeria, Syria, Pakistan, Australia, and Bulgaria?

I love it this way. There is nothing contrived or planned here—kind of like prayer. Prayer is a conversation between us and our creator, and we control only the part that comes from our lips and hearts. The other half of the dialogue is out of our hands. God's part of prayer is something that *happens* to us. I learned that God's part of prayer can happen while I'm sitting in a coffee shop with someone sharing prayer stories. And sometimes prayer is a text on my phone or it walks up to my front door.

Door to Door

I was sitting on my front porch on a warm August evening, reading a spiritual book, and mildly shooing the chipmunks scurrying under my chair. My new way of being allowed for moments like this, and I was savoring it. A couple of nicely dressed young men approached, lugging literature in shoulder bags. They stopped a polite distance away, just off the cement slab, and inquired if I was familiar with the salvation that came from reading the Bible.

I smiled, nodded, closed my book, and gave them my attention. They took turns explaining that they were college students selling religious books for the Bible Story Company as a means of financing their educations. They showed me the books and encouraged me to read excerpts. I looked at the first book, turned it over and read the back cover, and handed it back to them.

The curly-haired young man asked, "Do you like to read spiritual books?"

"Well, yes. Not only do I read them, I *write* spiritual books."

"Oh!" he replied. "Um . . . what kind?"

I explained my books briefly and said, "Currently, I am writing a book about family prayer. You wouldn't have any stories for me, would you?"

The straight-haired one shrugged, looked away, and said, "The rest of my family doesn't pray. They aren't religious." Then he walked away down the sidewalk. His friend watched him leave and turned back to me.

"Actually, my mom is praying for me right now."

"She is?" I said. "Why is that?"

He smiled shyly. "She worries about how people will treat me going door-to-door selling Christian books."

"Ah."

"Yeah . . ."

I asked, "And how are you being treated?"

His face brightened. "I think I am being treated very well. People are kind, even if they don't want to hear about the books. Really, it's fine. She shouldn't worry so much."

I ended up buying a vegetarian cookbook from him that was produced by the Seventh Day Adventists. My young, curly-haired canvasser turned out to be a computer science major at Andrews University in southwestern Michigan. He was polite, gentle, and good at his job. I asked if I could put him and his praying mother in my book, and he was perfectly fine with that.

God's part of the conversation delights me.

Holy Water

Nancy and I met because of our common interests in both social justice issues and writing. We can talk for hours about those two things. One day, while we were sipping coffee, she told me this story about praying for her granddaughter, Penelope. I asked her if she would write it for this book with the permission of her family. I love Nancy's definition of holy water.

I talk and even listen to God on a regular basis. It is like breathing; it just happens. Until it doesn't.

Two years ago, a tsunami pushed me into a corner of the Neonatal Intensive Care Unit (NICU) without the ability to move. My left foot was broken, but that problem paled in comparison to the fact that I was there watching my newborn granddaughter die.

I couldn't run away. Heck, I couldn't even walk without the clumsy use of crutches. So, I sat. I listened to silence. I watched my daughter grieve. And I cradled precious Penelope in my arms, hoping only to memorize her soft skin and peace-filled face.

I live by the adage that *when the going gets tough, the tough get going.* Under such circumstances, I pray harder and more frequently; I hold my rosary and sit before the Blessed Sacrament; I plead and I beg. In times of trouble it's common for me to mop my floor or weed my garden because I feel closest to God when I'm on the ground. I held Penelope for twenty days and did none of these things. Instead, I sat still, hour after hour, holding vigil.

I didn't say my usual prayers, and I think I lost my rosary. I made it to Mass only one time and when I heard the Advent song, "Joy to the World," I thought about walking out. It was strange to feel so disconnected from God. Part of me felt guilty; the other part didn't care.

I used the language of tears to pray. I cried each day, whenever I was alone. It reminded me that I was human and that bearing witness to loss is a form of vulnerability. "Jesus wept" (John 11:35) is not only the shortest Bible verse; it's where I go during times of sorrow. When words fail and faith falters, tears become my holy water.

My ninety-one-year-old mom reminded me that prayer time is not just about asking for a specific outcome. To her, in its purest form, it's about letting go and believing that God will give us what we need in all situations. I look back on my time with Penelope and now know that Jesus and I wept together. It's what I needed.

Tears are prayer in its purest form—they are, indeed, holy water. Nancy helped me see that "Jesus wept" is God by our side when the worst happens. On your prayer list today, write your sadness to God.

28

Two Toms

I first met Tom G. because he was my daughter's high-school religion teacher. I was a volunteer at the St. Vincent de Paul thrift store, and we needed young people to help us with delivering furniture, so I asked Tom if he had any ideas for recruiting strong, young talent. Before a month was out, he organized a winter-coat drive, invited me to speak to his classes, and came downtown to the store with a group of students. It was the beginning of a long and joy-filled collaboration between the school and the Society of St. Vincent de Paul. His unquenchable faith, combined with a love for teenagers, led me to assume that he had always been this way. However, against all odds, Tom has a tumbling faith history that veered from spiritual apathy, to all-consuming anger, to desperate, shouting-out-loud prayer.

I was born in September 1951, baptized Catholic a month later, and toted to church most Sundays until I was twelve. The Mass was in Latin in those days, and I saw it as an hour to kill. My dad seldom came with Mom, my brother, and me, and we were never taught any catechism that I can recall. We lived on a farm, and one Sunday, Mom said to me, "You can either come to church with me or work with Dad." I loved driving the tractor, so that was the easiest decision of my life. All through high school, I attended church for an occasional wedding or funeral and that was the extent of it.

In college I met Lois, my future wife. She had attended eleven years of Catholic school, and her parents were regular churchgoers. When we began dating, Lois gradually stopped going to church. I guess I was a negative influence because my view of faith was that it was a waste of time. At age twenty-four, we were married at the courthouse and didn't even invite our parents to come. As it turned out, my best man didn't show up, so we had the court secretary act as the witness and sign the papers. Lois giggled through the whole ceremony, and as we left I joked with her, "I don't think that judge gives us three weeks!" We were true hippies.

During the first year of our marriage, I began teaching history at the local high school. One day, after school ended, I walked out to the parking lot and started my car. The radio was on and the local news was playing. The announcer said, "Tom Rawlings got the shock of his life today when he died from electrocution while working on a billboard."

Tom Rawlings was my best friend.

We had known each other since kindergarten. He was gentle, funny, and giant hearted, and this callous newsman had just made a pun out of his horrific death. I don't know how I drove the car home. I shouldn't have been driving in the state I was in.

I charged into the house in a rage. I went nuts, smashed a chair, shouted every blasphemy I could think of, and watched Lois skitter away so as not to get too close to me. I called God—to his face—every despicable name that exists. I didn't know if he was out there, but if he was, I wanted him to know he had made the worst mistake in the universe.

A few days later, the minister stood up at the funeral home service to give the eulogy. In disbelief, I heard him begin his talk with, "Tom Rawlings got the shock of his life today when he died . . ."

I thought I was going to explode.

The preacher went on from there to explain that the horrific news had come to the entire community in this heartless way, upsetting everyone. "But," he said, "that announcer was exactly right. Tom went from the living side of life to the other side of life in the snap of a finger." Then the minister went on to talk about life after death and the hope that comes from faith.

I calmed down enough to stay sitting in my chair, but his words gave no comfort to me. In fact, I think they kept me from going to church for another ten years. If God was the one who had taken Tom out of this world into another one, then I didn't have any desire to talk to a being who would do a thing like that to such a good person.

Well, move on seven years. It was 1983, and Lois and I had lasted way past the three weeks predicted. We had two daughters and were at the hospital, expecting our third child, but the labor wasn't progressing well this time. The heartbeat was irregular, and there was a green discharge. The doctor told me that we had to do something. He was a Muslim, a man of faith, and I distinctly recall him putting the decision before me like this:

"Tom, one of four things is going to happen here: we may save the child but lose the mother; we may save the mother but lose the child; we may lose both of them; or we may save both of them. That's where we are. Will you give me permission to do a cesarean?"

I talked to Lois, and we gave him the go-ahead. He said to us, "I'll do my very best."

They wheeled Lois into the operating room, and I literally ran down the stairs to the prayer room. It was a small country hospital, and the prayer room was the size of a restroom. I went down on my hands and knees, palms to the floor. "God, I don't even know if you're out there, but if you are, save my wife and child! I don't know how you work, but if for some reason you need somebody—take me instead." I completely meant what I was saying and actually accepted that I might not get up off that floor, that God might take me at my word and I would be gone as instantly as my friend Tom Rawlings.

As soon as I made that prayer, a profound peace came over me. I had never been that peaceful in my entire life. It was almost a giddy feeling of happiness. I leapt up, ran out of the room, and took the steps two at a time to the second floor. Walking down the hallway was the doctor. I said to him, "Doc—let's do this!"

He grinned at me and said, "Where have you been? Mom and baby are fine. It's all taken care of. Come see them."

Immediate relief and ecstatic happiness and, at the same time—*Oh, shit. Did I just give God my life?* I realized that I had jumped in with both feet and couldn't back out.

Lois and I were both in. I suspect she may have been sneaking around saying the rosary a few times leading up to this moment, but after the scare we had, she was as converted as I was. We began going to Mass, then we had baby Lauren baptized, and, not too long after that, we got married in the church. We invited our parents this time. We had experienced a marvelous conversion, but . . . God wasn't finished.

Eight years later, April 20, 1991, we live in a country home across the road from my parents. The three girls are growing, and Lois and I are in love and still proving the judge wrong. It's Saturday, and Lauren is playing at her grandparents' house while I am behind their home cutting firewood with a chainsaw. At our house, Lois picks up the phone and calls my mom to tell her that she will be over to get Lauren to take her mushroom hunting. "Tell her I will meet her at the street." Our country road is narrow, with a speed limit of 55 mph, so we always had the rule that the kids could not cross it by themselves. They weren't allowed even to fetch the mail by themselves. Lois puts on her shoes and walks out the front door just as she hears the screech of tires and a loud thump. From the back of my parents' house, I hear the noises, too, and then Lois's scream. I think someone has hit our dog, who has a tendency to stand in the middle of the road, so I drop the saw and tear around the house.

Lois and I run to the road, and there is Lauren, lying on her side, eyes wide open, clothes nearly torn off, with a gaping wound on her right side above her pelvic bone. It is four inches long, and I can see her intestines. The thing is horrible, but what is more horrible is that it isn't bleeding. I put my fingers on both sides of her throat, searching for a pulse. I listen to her chest, check her armpits and wrists—*nothing*. By now, two other cars have stopped, the driver of the car that hit her is hysterical, and all the neighbors and family have run out to us. Lauren is not breathing, has no heartbeat, and all I know to do is to pull her into my arms, cradle her head in my elbow, and place my other hand on her chest, begging God to bring her back.

One of the cars turns around and drives like crazy to the nearest village a half mile away, finds the policeman, and sounds the alarm for an ambulance and paramedics. Four officers arrive very quickly: two state police and two county deputies. They all check for a pulse without success, but no one starts CPR.

Ten minutes after the accident, Lauren is still not breathing; the paramedics arrive and search fruitlessly for vital signs. I believe that the ambulance was called for a "dead on arrival" and, accordingly, they were traveling the speed limit without lights or siren. It's now fifteen minutes since Lauren was struck.

Lois is kneeling beside me, and about twenty people are gathered close around. She stands up and walks over to the driver, puts an arm around her shaking shoulders and says, "It's all right, it's all right. We

forgive you." Then she walks back to us and kneels down again, saying out loud, "Lord, you told us about a woman who wanted justice
from an unfair judge who ignored her, but she kept asking. Jesus said
we should always keep asking like that woman. That's what we are
doing now."

I said, "If only for a couple of minutes, Lord, so she knows her
mommy and daddy are here holding her. God, I ask you to send the
Holy Spirit. I would like you to enter her body and fix it in any way
you want to." I knew when I spoke those words that he might want
to fix her by taking her straight to heaven like my friend Tom.

Here's where the story gets interesting.

Lauren's body is cradled in my right arm; my left palm is on her
chest over her heart. That hand suddenly becomes very hot. It's so
hot, it's like a friction burn or like the sun on your face at the beach.
Definitely hot but not painful, *and it's coming from her.* She gasps
twice, then takes two strong breaths. I have been present when people
are dying, and I know that a last, gasping breath is normal. But I have
never heard *two* last breaths. About twenty people standing around us
watch her take those breaths and then keep breathing.

I look up at the police officer, and he gapes back at me, then turns
to his car and pulls the radio microphone out the window. "Where
the hell is that ambulance!" he says with conviction. I heard later,
from a friend who was following the ambulance, that suddenly they
went from 55 mph to over 80.

They scream up to us and within minutes have her on board.
Lois and I ride with her to the hospital. There is no messing around
with bandages or splints, no CPR (she is breathing now), and I can't
remember them doing anything with the wound except covering it. I
think they start an IV, and we arrive at the hospital forty-five minutes
after the accident.

The people at the desk say to me, "Sir, please come over here to fill out some paperwork," but my nephew takes my wallet out of my back pocket and shoves me into the ER with Lauren and Lois. "I'll do the paperwork," he says. They put Lauren in a cubicle and pull a curtain in front of our faces while a hoard of people rush over to work on her. We are standing there listening to what is going on when our parish priest, Fr. John, walks in. He says to the nurse, "How is the little girl doing?" The nurse takes him behind the curtain and I hear her say, "Not going to make it, Father." He administers the last rites of the church, and Lois and I are still standing on the outside.

The doctors order X-rays, which they take, but they all come out blurry, which no one can explain. The decision is made to order a helicopter from the city, forty miles away. Lois says to me, "It will take some time for the chopper to get here, so I'll stay. Meanwhile, your brother can drive you to the hospital, and you'll get there at about the same time they arrive. If she dies here, I'll be with her, and if she dies there, you'll be with her."

And Lois is right; we arrive just as they are taking her off the landing pad. They put her in ICU and it's touch and go. They do multiple scans, which show no broken bones at all. Later, we found out that the car was totaled. The radiator went through the engine fan and the paint was popped off the hood in a zigzag pattern all the way from the bumper to the windshield. From the place of impact to where Lauren landed was measured off by the police at seventy-seven feet.

The brain scan is not so miraculous. It shows two rips in the hypothalamus with active bleeding. The doctors decide that the next twenty-four hours will tell them how much damage was done. They tell us that all kinds of things can happen when that part of the brain is involved. We can expect anything from loss of major functions, to personality changes, to death. They close the wound in her side but the brain they leave alone for now. Lois and I wait by her side all night, praying.

In the morning, exactly at daybreak, Lauren opens her eyes. The nurse drops the tray she is carrying and runs out into the hall, calling for the doctor. He comes immediately and examines Lauren, shining his light into her eyes and talking to her. He meets her gaze and says to her, pointing at Lois, "Do you know who this is?"

Lauren says, "Uh-huh."

"Who is it?"

"Grandpa."

I thought, *Oh boy, we got problems.*

But the doctor stands up straight and says one word, "Miraculous." Then he walks out of the room.

Lauren knows who her mom is soon enough. She needs therapy to learn how to walk again, to relearn how to use the bathroom, and to regain other functions, but the accident happened in April, and our little girl makes rapid progress and is able to go back to school before the year is out.

I realized the minute she started to recover that, one day, Lauren will die. That's just the way it is. It's not morbid and it's not depressing. It only means that life is meant to be enjoyed, now, today.

Six years later, I go on a pilgrimage to a little town in Bosnia called Medjugorje, where it is said that the Virgin Mary has appeared to five teenagers. I spend time there in front of the Blessed Sacrament, praying for everyone I know. Every week, at church, I always say a prayer for my friend Tom, so of course I pray for him in Medjugorje, too. The moment I do that, the exact same peace comes over me as the one that covered me long ago, the day Lauren was born, when I was hands and knees to the floor in that tiny hospital prayer room. Every week for years, I have prayed for Tom, but this is the only time I have felt this peace.

The peace tells me quite clearly that Tom is okay.

I walk out of that chapel grinning. I still don't know *why* Tom had to go, but I now accept that he did. *And it is okay.*

On my family prayer list there is always a plea for a miracle or two: someone with untreatable cancer or someone who is unexplainably angry—those Hail Mary tosses of the football on the last play of the game. Sometimes, I am afraid to ask for the miracle. Why is that? The story of the two Toms tells me that it could go either way, and Tom knows this better than anyone. His beloved Lois passed away from a brain tumor shortly before retirement. Several years later, he shared his story with me over a cup of coffee with his new wife, Donna, at his side.

✎ **If you are ready, go ahead and put a miracle prayer on your list today.**

29

Praying with a
Mother's Heart

Gretchen has been on my prayer list for just one year. Not Gretchen exactly—her whole family—but Gretchen especially. She is my Zumba instructor, a natural dancer who loves to instruct and encourage inflexible, middle-aged, flat-footed people like me in balance, rhythm, and the joy of moving our feet, hips, and shoulders. I signed up for her class to help cure my back spasms, and it worked. She is unquenchably cheerful, kindhearted, and patient. I love her Zumba class, and I love her.

Her youngest son, Dan, was diagnosed with leukemia when he was still a teen, but he battled it into remission. When I first met Gretchen, Dan was twenty-five, engaged to be married, and bursting with health. Last year, weeks after the wedding, the leukemia came back. Sadly, this is not a miracle story of how prayer defeated the terrible disease; Dan passed away before celebrating his first anniversary with lovely Sarah. This is, however, a story of family prayer. It takes place about six weeks after Dan's passing.

My husband and I have contributed to St. Jude's Research Hospital for years. In their thank-you letters they send us photos of their patients, little children with bald heads and bruised arms. I can't throw these pictures away, so I put them in a photo album, just as if they were kids I know personally. From time to time, I go through the album and pray for the children and their parents. My little grandson, Dan's nephew, for some reason, loves to go through this book, too. When I am babysitting, he will pull it off the shelf and bring it to me, and we pray for the young patients together.

Several weeks after Dan passed away, I was having one of those bad days where the grief was working on me and I wasn't holding things together very well. When the thoughts of "What if?" or "If only . . ." or "What's next?" won't give way to Bible verses about God's love, I find it hard to be myself. On this particular day, I was babysitting, and, as usual, the St. Jude album came off the shelf and was plunked in my lap.

"Okay," I said, though I didn't much feel like looking at children sick with cancer. "Let's pray for the kids." And we did, and what came to me as we paged through the photos was this: *some of these are just babies, and most haven't finished grade school. How do their parents deal with it?*

And the grateful thought hit me that Dan had survived childhood. We were able to raise him, watch him graduate, dance at his wedding, and love his beautiful Sarah.

So much joy.

And yes, so much sorrow in watching him suffer and in losing him. But the little ones in the St. Jude's book have families who might never see those milestone days. I am blessed to be able to pray for them with a mother's heart that knows the pain they are facing. Perhaps that is how God is beginning to heal me—through praying for other children and their families, with my grandson tucked in my arms praying with me.

Gretchen's prayer list of photos broke my heart. Perhaps all prayer lists are supposed to do that. Prayers that break our hearts are the way into God's heart.

> My sacrifice, O God, is a broken spirit; a broken and contrite heart you, God, will not despise.
>
> —Psalm 51:17

Epilogue

I am struck by how often the conclusion of these stories was similar. No matter how heart wrenching—especially when prayers seemed to go unanswered—the ultimate realization for many people was: "And I knew it was okay." By this, they did not mean that everything was back to the way it had been, nor did they mean that their prayers had been answered perfectly. Instead, they used the unchurchy word *okay*.

My family prayer list helped me during three hard years that Dean and I endured. The list gave our prayers a focus other than ourselves. Along the way, the prayers for other people that were answered gave me reasons to rejoice and to hope that my problems would find solutions, too. Praying for others helped me put my own worries in perspective and gave me a shattering sense of gratitude.

All the troubles didn't cause me to fall apart, but I don't ever want to get any closer.

Yet, I too, after falling into prayer, know for certain that "it is okay."

This language is not something quoted from Scripture, memorized from a formal prayer, or read in a devotional. None of the people in these stories told me, "God helps those that help themselves," "God won't give you more than you can handle," or "What doesn't kill you makes you stronger." The stories in this book are from ordinary people floating in the rough ocean of life, and their family prayers were flung out in all directions like droplets from a kiddie swimming pool.

This is how they prayed: "It's like riding a bicycle." "I tried to find an obscure corner where I would not be seen." "Jesus needs it." "Do not worry about the war." "Mom, you gotta have faith." "God, make him strong and good." "You will be crying." "Mama Mary, wrap us in your mantel." "You're going to heaven!" "Get down on your knees." "I don't even like you." "He is the God of fifty-nine minutes and fifty-nine seconds." "She was wearing a blue dress!" "Do you want to dance?" "I always hoped you would be successful." "Jesus wept." "Oh shit—did I just give my life to God?" "Okay . . . let's pray for the kids."

Over and over again, they told me, "I knew it was okay." This is not an "okay" of resignation. It is an awareness of peace. *And what brought them that peace was prayer.*

There is one last quote for me to ponder—it is important because this book is about family prayer, and this came from the man whose family had fallen apart. He had lost his peace and his joy. He did not blame it on bad luck, on other people, or on tragedy. He blamed his loss on himself because he had ceased to pray when times were good.

"Don't ever stop praying," he told me.

I am so grateful I listened.

Acknowledgments

Joe Durepos walked me through this book. He envisioned it long before I did, and he gave me the confidence to attempt writing it. I am so grateful.

Vinita Hampton Wright and Katherine Faydash were my careful editors, and they made the sentences flow. I am blessed to receive your advice. All the good people at Loyola Press have my gratitude for their work on this book, from the cover to the formatting issues, from the title to the enthusiastic marketing plan—you are the best!

My friends and family who shared their stories with me over the past few months were generous to an extreme in revealing their deepest experiences of family prayer. This book is theirs more than it is mine. Thank you for being part of it.

Dean, Martha, and Ginny were valuable readers of the manuscript. *The Prayer List* might have been a random series of stories without their input. I am thankful for the time each of you took to read and advise me.

And, last, Dean, Ellen, and Martha pray with me a lot. Thank you for praying for all these years. This book would not exist but for that.

About the Author

Jane Knuth is a longtime volunteer for the St. Vincent de Paul Society in Kalamazoo, Michigan. In 2011, Jane's first book, *Thrift Store Saints*, was awarded first place from the Catholic Press Association for Popular Presentation of the Catholic Faith. She also writes a monthly column for *The Good News*, the newspaper of the Diocese of Kalamazoo. She and her husband, Dean, live in Portage, Michigan, and have two daughters, Ellen and Martha.

Also by Jane Knuth

Thrift Store Saints
Meeting Jesus 25¢ at a Time

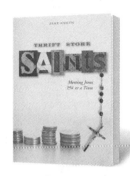

Thrift Store Saints is a collection of true stories based on Jane Knuth's experiences and personal transformation serving the poor at a St. Vincent de Paul thrift store in Kalamazoo, Michigan.

978-0-8294-3301-2 | PB | $13.95

Thrift Store Graces
Finding God's Gifts in the Midst of the Mess

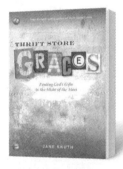

Jane Knuth returns with more stories as a once reluctant, now enthusiastic volunteer. She introduces us to some far more challenging personal situations and demonstrates that some of God's greatest gifts come disguised as difficulties.

978-0-8294-3692-1 | PB | $13.95

Love Will Steer Me True
A Mother and Daughter's Conversations on Life, Love, and God

Delightfully conversational and inviting, Love Will Steer Me True shows how a mother and daughter swerve and weave their way into a new understanding of themselves, of their familial relationship, and of their faith.

978-0-8294-4143-7 | PB | $13.95

To Order:
Call **800.621.1008**, visit **loyolapress.com/store,** or visit your local bookseller.